S.P DEVDAS

Psychology

Growth think

Contents

1

Introduction to Psychological Growth

Psychological growth is a fascinating journey that unfolds throughout our lives, shaping who we are and how we perceive the world around us. At its core, psychological growth encompasses the intricate processes of cognitive, emotional, social, and spiritual development that occur from infancy to old age. It is a multifaceted phenomenon influenced by a myriad of factors, including genetics, environment, culture, and individual experiences.

Understanding psychological growth is essential for comprehending human behavior and the complexities of the human mind. It allows us to explore how individuals evolve over time, how they navigate through various life stages, and how they adapt to the challenges and opportunities presented by their environments.

In this introductory chapter, we will embark on a journey to explore the foundations of psychological growth. We will delve into the key theories and concepts that underpin our understanding of development, from early childhood to adulthood and beyond. By examining the biological, cognitive, social, and emotional aspects of growth, we will uncover the intricate interplay between nature and nurture in shaping human development.

Throughout this exploration, we will encounter the rich diversity of human experiences and the universal themes that connect us all. From the joys of childhood exploration to the complexities of adult relationships, psychological growth encompasses a wide range of phenomena that shape our identities and influence our interactions with the world.

As we delve deeper into the realm of psychological growth, we will discover the profound impact it has on our well-being, relationships, and sense of self. We will explore the factors that contribute to resilience and adaptation in the face of adversity, as well as the challenges that can hinder our growth and development.

Ultimately, our journey into psychological growth is not just an academic pursuit but a deeply personal one. It invites us to reflect on our own experiences of growth and transformation, and to consider how we can foster positive development in ourselves and others. By embracing the journey of psychological growth, we embark on a path of self-discovery, fulfillment, and lifelong learning.

Psychological growth encompasses the myriad processes through which individuals evolve, adapt, and transform across the lifespan. Rooted in the intricate interplay between biological, cognitive, emotional, social, and environmental factors, psychological growth is a fundamental aspect of human development. From infancy to old age, individuals navigate through various stages, confronting challenges, forging connections, and acquiring new skills that shape their identities and trajectories.

This introductory chapter sets the stage for exploring the dynamic nature of psychological growth. We delve into the foundational theories, methodologies, and key concepts that underpin our understanding of human development. From Freud's psychoanalytic perspective to Erikson's psychosocial stages, and from Piaget's cognitive theory to modern neuroscientific insights, we embark on a journey through the rich tapestry of developmental psychology.

Moreover, this chapter elucidates the significance of psychological growth in fostering resilience, well-being, and fulfillment. By examining the complexities of nature versus nurture, individual differences, and cultural influences, we gain insights into the diverse pathways of growth that individuals traverse. Through a multidimensional lens, we explore how relationships, experiences, and societal contexts shape our perceptions, behaviors, and sense of self.

Furthermore, this introductory exploration sets the stage for delving into the intricate nuances of psychological growth across the lifespan. From the innocence and wonder of childhood to the tumultuous transitions of adolescence, and from the challenges and opportunities of adulthood to the reflections and adaptations of old age, we illuminate the multifaceted nature of human development.

In essence, this introductory chapter serves as a gateway to understanding the complexities, wonders, and mysteries of psychological growth. As we embark on this journey, we invite readers to engage in introspection, inquiry, and dialogue, fostering a deeper appreciation for the remarkable journey of human development.

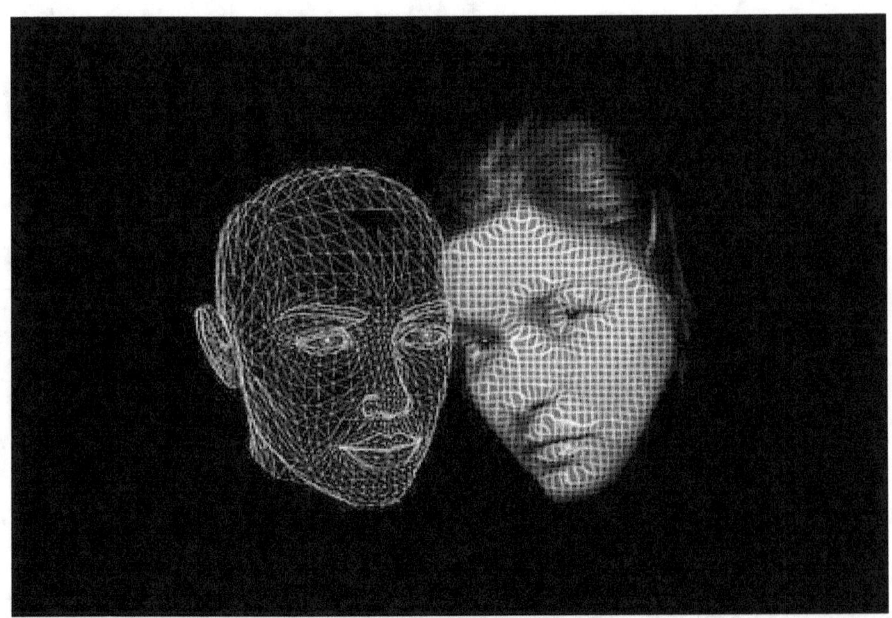

2

2

Foundations of Developmental Psychology

Developmental psychology serves as the bedrock upon which our understanding of human growth and change is built. This branch of psychology investigates how individuals evolve physically, cognitively, emotionally, and socially from conception through adulthood and beyond. At its core, developmental psychology seeks to unravel the intricate interplay between nature and nurture, exploring the genetic, biological, environmental, and experiential factors that shape human development.

One of the foundational pillars of developmental psychology is the notion of continuity and discontinuity in development. Continuity suggests that development is a gradual, cumulative process, where skills and abilities build upon each other over time. Conversely, discontinuity posits that development occurs in distinct stages, marked by qualitative shifts in behavior and understanding. Through longitudinal studies, cross-sectional analyses, and mixed-method approaches, researchers endeavor to unravel the complex dynamics of continuity and discontinuity in human development.

Another cornerstone of developmental psychology is the study of critical and sensitive periods. Critical periods represent windows of heightened plasticity during which specific experiences have a profound and enduring impact on development. For instance, the early years of life are marked by critical periods for language acquisition, social bonding, and sensory-motor development. In contrast, sensitive periods denote periods of increased susceptibility to environmental influences, where certain skills or behaviors are more readily shaped by experience.

Furthermore, developmental psychology explores the role of individual differences in shaping developmental trajectories. From genetic predispositions to environmental contexts, from cultural norms to familial dynamics, myriad factors contribute to the rich tapestry of human diversity. Through twin studies, adoption studies, and behavioral genetics research, psychologists unravel the intricate interplay between genetic predispositions and environmental influences in shaping individual differences in development.

Moreover, developmental psychology delves into the concept of resilience, examining how individuals navigate through adversity and thrive in the face of challenges. By investigating protective factors, coping mechanisms, and positive adaptations, researchers shed light on the factors that promote resilience and well-being across the lifespan.

In essence, the foundations of developmental psychology provide a comprehensive framework for understanding the complexities, wonders, and mysteries of human development. By unraveling the intricate interplay between nature and nurture, continuity and discontinuity, and individual differences and resilience, developmental psychologists illuminate the remarkable journey of growth and change that defines the human experience.

Developmental psychology, as a discipline, seeks to unravel the intricate processes of growth, change, and adaptation that characterize human development. At its core, developmental psychology explores how individuals evolve physically, cognitively, emotionally, and socially from conception to death. To comprehend the essence of this field, it's essential to explore its foundational principles, theories, and methodologies.

One of the cornerstone principles of developmental psychology is the belief in the continuity of development. This principle posits that development is a continuous and cumulative process, where earlier experiences and influences lay the groundwork for subsequent growth. From the prenatal period, where the foundations of neural circuitry are laid, to the complex interactions of adulthood, developmental psychologists study how individuals build upon prior experiences to navigate new challenges.

Another fundamental principle is the notion of nature versus nurture. This age-old debate examines the relative contributions of genetic predispositions (nature) and environmental influences (nurture) in shaping human development. While acknowledging the interplay between genetics and environment, developmental psychologists investigate how inherited traits interact with environmental stimuli to influence behavior, cognition, and personality.

Furthermore, developmental psychology is deeply rooted in various theoretical frameworks that offer insights into the mechanisms and stages of development. Sigmund Freud's psychosexual theory, Jean Piaget's cognitive developmental theory, Erik Erikson's psychosocial theory, and Lev Vygotsky's sociocultural theory are among the influential paradigms that have shaped our understanding of human development. These theories provide lenses through which researchers examine the cognitive, emotional, and social dimensions of growth across the lifespan.

Methodologically, developmental psychologists employ a diverse array of research methods to investigate human development. Longitudinal studies track individuals over time, providing valuable insights into developmental trajectories and continuity. Cross-sectional studies compare different age groups at a single point in time, offering snapshots of developmental differences. Experimental designs, observational studies, and case studies complement these approaches, enriching our understanding of the intricate processes of development.

In summary, the foundations of developmental psychology are built upon principles of continuity, nature versus nurture, and theoretical frameworks that illuminate the complexities of human development. By employing a variety of research methods, developmental psychologists unravel the mysteries of growth, shedding light on the remarkable journey from infancy to old age.

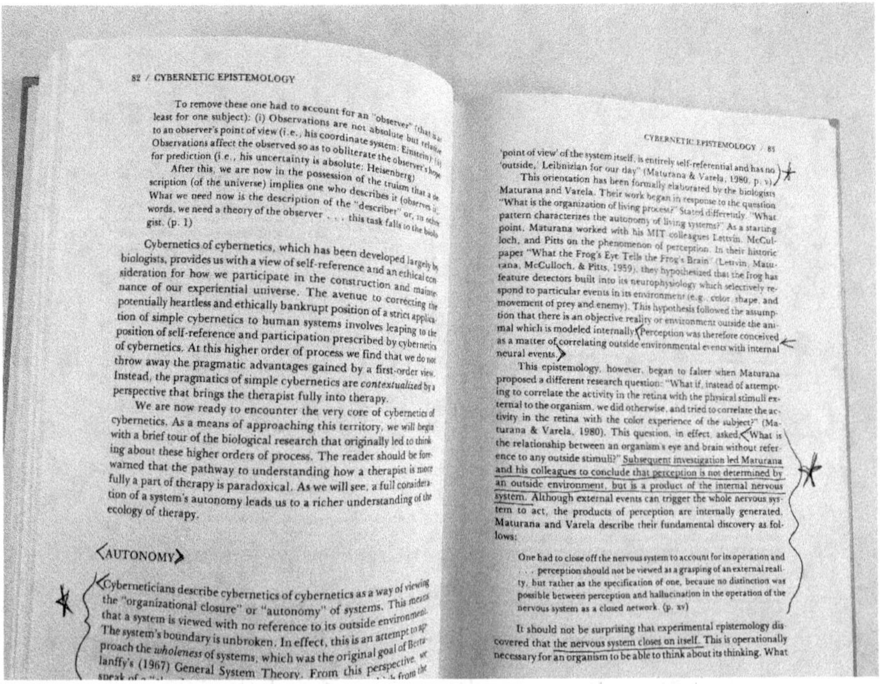

To remove these one had to account for an "observer" (that is, at least for one subject): (i) Observations are not absolute but relative to an observer's point of view (i.e., his coordinate system: Einstein) (ii) Observations affect the observed so as to obliterate the observer's hope for prediction (i.e., his uncertainty is absolute: Heisenberg)

After this, we are now in the possession of the truism that a description (of the universe) implies one who describes it (observes it). What we need now is the description of the "describer" or, in other words, we need a theory of the observer . . . this task falls to the biologist. (p. 1)

Cybernetics of cybernetics, which has been developed largely by biologists, provides us with a view of self-reference and an ethical consideration for how we participate in the construction and maintenance of our experiential universe. The avenue to correcting the potentially heartless and ethically bankrupt position of a strict application of simple cybernetics to human systems involves leaping to the position of self-reference and participation prescribed by cybernetics of cybernetics. At this higher order of process we find that we do not throw away the pragmatic advantages gained by a first-order view. Instead, the pragmatics of simple cybernetics are *contextualized* by a perspective that brings the therapist fully into therapy.

We are now ready to encounter the very core of cybernetics of cybernetics. As a means of approaching this territory, we will begin with a brief tour of the biological research that originally led to thinking about these higher orders of process. The reader should be forewarned that the pathway to understanding how a therapist is more fully a part of therapy is paradoxical. As we will see, a full consideration of a system's autonomy leads us to a richer understanding of the ecology of therapy.

AUTONOMY

Cyberneticians describe cybernetics of cybernetics as a way of viewing the "organizational closure" or "autonomy" of systems. This means that a system is viewed with no reference to its outside environment. The system's boundary is unbroken. In effect, this is an attempt to approach the *wholeness* of systems, which was the original goal of Bertalanffy's (1967) General System Theory. From this perspective, we speak of a "whole" . . . from the

'point of view' of the system itself, is entirely self-referential and has no 'outside,' Leibnizian for our day" (Maturana & Varela, 1980, p. v).

This orientation has been formally elaborated by the biologists Maturana and Varela. Their work began in response to the question "What is the organization of living process?" Stated differently, "What pattern characterizes the autonomy of living systems?" As a starting point, Maturana worked with his MIT colleagues Lettvin, McCulloch, and Pitts on the phenomenon of perception. In their historic paper "What the Frog's Eye Tells the Frog's Brain" (Lettvin, Maturana, McCulloch, & Pitts, 1959), they hypothesized that the frog has feature detectors built into its neurophysiology which selectively respond to particular events in its environment (e.g., color, shape, and movement of prey and enemy). This hypothesis followed the assumption that there is an objective reality or environment outside the animal which is modeled internally. Perception was therefore conceived as a matter of correlating outside environmental events with internal neural events.

This epistemology, however, began to falter when Maturana proposed a different research question: "What if, instead of attempting to correlate the activity in the retina with the physical stimuli external to the organism, we did otherwise, and tried to correlate the activity in the retina with the color experience of the subject?" (Maturana & Varela, 1980). This question, in effect, asked, What is the relationship between an organism's eye and brain without reference to any outside stimuli?" Subsequent investigation led Maturana and his colleagues to conclude that perception is not determined by an outside environment, but is a product of the internal nervous system. Although external events can trigger the whole nervous system to act, the products of perception are internally generated. Maturana and Varela describe their fundamental discovery as follows:

> One had to close off the nervous system to account for its operation and . . . perception should not be viewed as a grasping of an external reality, but rather as the specification of one, because no distinction was possible between perception and hallucination in the operation of the nervous system as a closed network. (p. xv)

It should not be surprising that experimental epistemology discovered that the nervous system closes on itself. This is operationally necessary for an organism to be able to think about its thinking. What

3

Theories of Psychological Growth

Psychological growth is a multifaceted phenomenon that has been theorized and studied by numerous scholars across various disciplines. Several prominent theorists have offered comprehensive frameworks to understand the complexities of human development. Among these theorists, Sigmund Freud, Erik Erikson, and Jean Piaget stand as pillars in the field of developmental psychology, each offering unique perspectives on psychological growth.

Sigmund Freud's psychoanalytic theory posits that human development is driven by unconscious motives and conflicts, particularly during childhood. According to Freud, personality is structured into three components: the id, ego, and superego. Freud's psychosexual stages of development, including the oral, anal, phallic, latent, and genital stages, highlight the significance of early childhood experiences in shaping personality and behavior. Freud's emphasis on the role of unconscious processes and early experiences in psychological growth revolutionized our understanding of human development.

Erik Erikson expanded upon Freud's work with his psychosocial theory of development. Erikson proposed that individuals navigate through a series of psychosocial crises across the lifespan, each representing a conflict between opposing needs or demands. From trust versus mistrust in infancy to integrity versus despair in old age, Erikson's eight stages of psychosocial development illustrate the interplay between internal maturation and external social influences. Erikson's theory emphasizes the importance of achieving a sense of identity and purpose in fostering psychological growth and well-being.

Jean Piaget, a pioneering cognitive psychologist, introduced the theory of cognitive development, which focuses on how children actively construct their understanding of the world through interaction with their environment. Piaget identified four stages of cognitive development: sensorimotor, preoperational, concrete operational, and formal operational. According to Piaget, children progress through these stages by assimilating new information into existing schemas and accommodating their schemas to incorporate new experiences. Piaget's theory highlights the qualitative shifts in thinking that occur as individuals progress from infancy to adolescence, shedding light on the underlying mechanisms of psychological growth.

Beyond Freud, Erikson, and Piaget, numerous other theorists have contributed to our understanding of psychological growth. Lev Vygotsky's sociocultural theory emphasizes the role of social interactions and cultural influences in cognitive development. Urie Bronfenbrenner's ecological systems theory underscores the importance of environmental contexts, such as family, school, and community, in shaping development. Each of these theories offers valuable insights into the intricate processes of psychological growth, enriching our understanding of the remarkable journey from infancy to adulthood.

A rich tapestry of theories has been woven by prominent psychologists to elucidate the mechanisms and stages of psychological growth across the lifespan. Among the most influential are the theories proposed by Sigmund Freud, Erik Erikson, and Jean Piaget, each offering unique perspectives on the intricacies of human development.

Sigmund Freud's psychoanalytic theory posits that personality development unfolds through a series of psychosexual stages: oral, anal, phallic, latency, and genital. According to Freud, conflicts and experiences during these stages shape personality traits and behaviors in adulthood. While Freud's emphasis on unconscious drives and early childhood experiences has garnered both acclaim and criticism, his theory remains a foundational framework in understanding the complexities of psychological growth.

Erik Erikson expanded upon Freud's work with his psychosocial theory, which emphasizes the importance of social relationships and cultural context in shaping identity development. Erikson proposed a series of psychosocial stages, each characterized by a developmental task or crisis that individuals must resolve. From trust versus mistrust in infancy to integrity versus despair in old age, Erikson's theory highlights the lifelong journey of identity formation and growth.

Jean Piaget's cognitive developmental theory revolutionized our understanding of how children perceive, reason, and make sense of the world. Piaget proposed a series of stages of cognitive development: sensorimotor, preoperational, concrete operational, and formal operational. According to Piaget, children actively construct their understanding of reality through processes such as assimilation and accommodation. His theory underscores the dynamic interplay between biological maturation and environmental experiences in shaping cognitive growth.

Furthermore, Lev Vygotsky's sociocultural theory emphasizes the role of social interactions, cultural tools, and historical context in cognitive development. Vygotsky proposed that learning occurs through social collaboration and scaffolding, wherein more knowledgeable others guide learners to higher levels of understanding. His theory highlights the significance of language, culture, and socialization in fostering cognitive growth and development.

In addition to these seminal theories, contemporary perspectives such as attachment theory, ecological systems theory, and resilience theory continue to enrich our understanding of psychological growth. Each theory offers valuable insights into the multifaceted nature of human development, illuminating the dynamic interplay of biological, cognitive, emotional, and social factors in shaping individuals' trajectories from infancy to old age.

4

4

Biological Basis of Psychological Growth

At the core of psychological growth lies a complex interplay between biological processes and psychological phenomena. Understanding the biological basis of psychological growth requires exploring the intricate workings of the brain, genetics, and the physiological systems that underpin human development.

The brain serves as the command center for psychological growth, orchestrating a myriad of functions that govern cognition, emotion, behavior, and perception. Within the brain, neurons communicate through intricate networks, forming the basis of learning, memory, and decision-making. Neurotransmitters and hormones regulate mood, motivation, and stress responses, influencing psychological well-being and resilience.

Furthermore, advances in neuroimaging techniques such as fMRI and EEG have enabled researchers to map the neural circuits associated with various aspects of psychological growth. From the development of language and executive functions in childhood to the decline of cognitive abilities in old age, neuroscientific research provides valuable insights into the biological underpinnings of human development.

Genetics also play a crucial role in psychological growth, shaping individual differences in temperament, personality, and susceptibility to mental health disorders. Through the interplay of genes and environment, genetic predispositions interact with environmental influences to shape psychological traits and behaviors. Twin and adoption studies have provided compelling evidence for the heritability of certain psychological characteristics, highlighting the role of genetics in shaping developmental trajectories.

Moreover, the physiological systems of the body, such as the endocrine and immune systems, contribute to psychological growth through their influence on stress regulation, health outcomes, and resilience. Chronic stress, for example, can dysregulate the hypothalamic-pituitary-adrenal (HPA) axis, leading to adverse effects on cognitive function, emotional well-being, and physical health.

In summary, the biological basis of psychological growth encompasses a vast array of intricate processes within the brain, genetics, and physiological systems. By unraveling the complexities of neural functioning, genetic predispositions, and physiological responses, researchers gain deeper insights into the mechanisms that underlie human development. Understanding the biological foundations of psychological growth not only informs theoretical frameworks but also has practical implications for promoting resilience, mental health, and well-being across the lifespan.

At the intersection of biology and psychology lies a profound understanding of how biological factors shape and influence psychological growth through-out the lifespan. From the intricate wiring of the brain to the interplay of genetics and environment, the biological basis of psychological growth offers invaluable insights into the complexities of human development.

Central to the biological basis of psychological growth is the structure and function of the brain. The brain, often described as the body's command center, undergoes remarkable changes from infancy to adulthood, sculpting neural circuits that underpin cognitive, emotional, and behavioral processes. Brain imaging techniques, such as functional magnetic resonance imaging (fMRI) and electroencephalography (EEG), enable researchers to explore how different regions of the brain contribute to various aspects of psychological functioning.

Moreover, genetic factors play a pivotal role in shaping psychological growth. Hereditary traits inherited from parents influence a myriad of characteristics, from temperament and personality to susceptibility to mental health disorders. Advances in molecular genetics have allowed researchers to identify specific genes associated with traits and behaviors, shedding light on the complex interplay between nature and nurture in human development.

Furthermore, the prenatal environment exerts a profound influence on psychological growth. From the moment of conception, a developing fetus is shaped by maternal nutrition, stress levels, and exposure to toxins. Teratogens, such as alcohol and drugs, can have lasting effects on brain development, leading to cognitive and behavioral impairments later in life. Understanding the prenatal origins of psychological growth underscores the importance of prenatal care and maternal well-being in fostering healthy development.

In addition to prenatal influences, early childhood experiences play a crucial role in shaping psychological growth. The quality of caregiving, attachment relationships, and environmental stimulation during the formative years profoundly impact brain development and emotional regulation. Adverse experiences, such as neglect or trauma, can disrupt neurobiological processes, leading to long-term consequences for mental health and well-being.

Furthermore, hormonal changes associated with puberty and adolescence contribute to psychological growth and identity formation. Fluctuations in hormones, such as testosterone and estrogen, influence mood, behavior, and social interactions during this transitional period. Understanding the biological underpinnings of adolescent development provides insights into the challenges and opportunities inherent in navigating the teenage years.

In summary, the biological basis of psychological growth underscores the intricate interplay between genetics, brain development, and environmental influences in shaping human development. By unraveling the complexities of biological factors, researchers gain a deeper understanding of the mechanisms underlying psychological growth, paving the way for interventions and strategies to promote optimal development and well-being across the lifespan.

5

5

Cognitive Development in Childhood

The journey of cognitive development in childhood is a remarkable process characterized by profound changes in how children perceive, reason, and make sense of the world around them. From the sensorimotor explorations of infancy to the increasingly complex thought processes of adolescence, cognitive development unfolds in stages, guided by biological maturation and environmental experiences.

Jean Piaget, a pioneering developmental psychologist, proposed a series of stages of cognitive development that provide a framework for understanding how children's thinking evolves over time. According to Piaget, children progress through four main stages: sensorimotor, preoperational, concrete operational, and formal operational.

During the sensorimotor stage (birth to age 2), infants engage in sensory exploration and motor activities to understand the world. They learn about object permanence—the understanding that objects continue to exist even when they are out of sight—and develop basic concepts of cause and effect through trial and error.

The preoperational stage (ages 2 to 7) is characterized by symbolic thinking and egocentrism. Children begin to use language and mental imagery to represent objects and events, but their thinking is still guided by intuition rather than logic. Egocentrism leads children to perceive the world solely from their own perspective, making it challenging for them to understand others' viewpoints.

In the concrete operational stage (ages 7 to 11), children acquire the ability to think logically about concrete objects and events. They can perform mental operations, such as conservation (understanding that quantity remains the same despite changes in appearance) and classification (sorting objects into categories based on shared characteristics). However, their thinking is limited to concrete, tangible experiences.

Finally, in the formal operational stage (ages 11 and beyond), adolescents develop the capacity for abstract and hypothetical thinking. They can reason logically about hypothetical situations, engage in deductive reasoning, and contemplate complex moral and philosophical concepts. This stage marks the emergence of higher-order thinking skills, enabling individuals to engage in scientific inquiry, critical analysis, and creative problem-solving.

In addition to Piaget's stages, contemporary research has expanded our understanding of cognitive development by highlighting the role of social interactions, cultural influences, and individual differences. Lev Vygotsky's sociocultural theory emphasizes the importance of social collaboration and cultural tools in scaffolding children's cognitive growth. According to Vygotsky, children learn through interactions with more knowledgeable others, who provide guidance and support to facilitate learning and problem-solving.

Furthermore, advances in neuroscience have deepened our understanding of brain development and its implications for cognitive functioning in childhood. Brain imaging studies reveal how different regions of the brain mature and specialize during childhood, influencing cognitive processes such as attention, memory, and executive function.

In summary, cognitive development in childhood is a multifaceted process shaped by biological maturation, environmental experiences, and social interactions. By understanding the stages and mechanisms of cognitive development, educators, caregivers, and policymakers can support children's learning and intellectual growth, laying the foundation for future success and fulfillment.

The journey of cognitive development in childhood is a fascinating exploration of how children perceive, reason, and understand the world around them. From the early sensorimotor explorations of infancy to the complex problem-solving abilities of adolescence, cognitive development unfolds in a series of stages, each characterized by distinct milestones and achievements.

Jean Piaget, a pioneer in the field of developmental psychology, proposed a seminal theory of cognitive development that continues to shape our understanding of childhood cognition. According to Piaget, children progress through four stages of cognitive development: the sensorimotor stage, the preoperational stage, the concrete operational stage, and the formal operational stage.

During the sensorimotor stage, which spans from birth to around age 2, infants learn about the world through sensory experiences and motor actions. They develop object permanence, the understanding that objects continue to exist even when they are out of sight, and begin to engage in simple problem-solving behaviors.

The preoperational stage, which typically occurs from ages 2 to 7, is marked by significant advances in language and symbolic thinking. Children in this stage engage in pretend play, use symbols to represent objects and events, and demonstrate egocentrism, the tendency to view the world from their own perspective.

In the concrete operational stage, which typically spans from ages 7 to 11, children become capable of more logical and systematic thinking. They can perform operations on concrete objects and understand concepts such as conservation, the understanding that certain properties of objects remain constant despite changes in their appearance.

Finally, in the formal operational stage, which emerges around age 11 and continues into adulthood, individuals develop the ability to think abstractly and hypothetically. They can engage in deductive reasoning, problem-solving, and hypothetical-deductive thinking, enabling them to grapple with complex concepts and ideas.

In addition to Piaget's theory, contemporary research has expanded our understanding of cognitive development in childhood. Insights from neuroscience, cognitive psychology, and educational psychology have illuminated the role of factors such as executive functions, working memory, and metacognition in shaping children's cognitive abilities.

Furthermore, socio-cultural perspectives highlight the importance of social interactions, cultural tools, and educational experiences in scaffolding children's cognitive development. Vygotsky's theory of sociocultural development emphasizes the role of social interactions and cultural context in shaping cognitive growth, underscoring the significance of guided participation and zone of proximal development in fostering learning and problem-solving skills.

In summary, cognitive development in childhood is a dynamic and multi-faceted process characterized by remarkable achievements and milestones. From the sensorimotor explorations of infancy to the abstract thinking of adolescence, children's cognitive abilities evolve in response to biological maturation, social experiences, and environmental influences, laying the foundation for future learning, reasoning, and problem-solving skills.

6

6

Social and Emotional Development in Childhood

Childhood is a critical period for the development of social and emotional competence, laying the foundation for healthy relationships, self-regulation, and well-being throughout life. From the earliest interactions with caregivers to the complexities of peer relationships, children navigate a rich tapestry of social and emotional experiences that shape their development.

Attachment theory, pioneered by John Bowlby and Mary Ainsworth, offers valuable insights into the early roots of social and emotional development. According to attachment theory, the quality of the bond between infants and caregivers profoundly influences children's sense of security, emotional regulation, and ability to form relationships later in life. Secure attachment provides a foundation for exploring the world, seeking comfort from caregivers, and developing a positive sense of self.

Throughout childhood, children's social and emotional development is characterized by significant milestones and challenges. During the early years, infants develop basic emotions such as joy, sadness, fear, and anger, learning to express and regulate their feelings in response to social cues and interactions. As children grow, they become increasingly capable of recognizing and understanding the emotions of others, a process known as empathy, which forms the basis of prosocial behavior and moral development.

Peer relationships play a crucial role in social and emotional development during childhood. From preschool playgroups to schoolyard friendships, children learn important social skills such as cooperation, sharing, and conflict resolution through interactions with peers. Peer acceptance and social competence become increasingly important during middle childhood, influencing children's self-esteem, sense of belonging, and overall well-being.

Moreover, the family environment profoundly shapes children's social and emotional development. Warm, supportive parenting fosters secure attachment and emotional resilience, while harsh or inconsistent parenting can undermine children's sense of safety and trust. Sibling relationships, family routines, and cultural values also influence children's socialization experiences, shaping their social skills, emotional expression, and identity development.

In addition to interpersonal relationships, children's social and emotional development is influenced by broader societal factors such as culture, community, and media. Cultural norms and values shape children's understanding of emotions, social roles, and relationships, influencing their socialization experiences and self-concept. Media exposure, including television, video games, and social media, can also impact children's social and emotional development, shaping their attitudes, behaviors, and perceptions of the world.

In summary, social and emotional development in childhood is a complex and dynamic process shaped by interactions between biological, psychological, and social factors. From the formation of early attachments to the complexities of peer relationships, children's social and emotional experiences lay the groundwork for healthy development and flourishing throughout life. Understanding the intricacies of social and emotional development in childhood is essential for promoting resilience, empathy, and well-being in future generations.

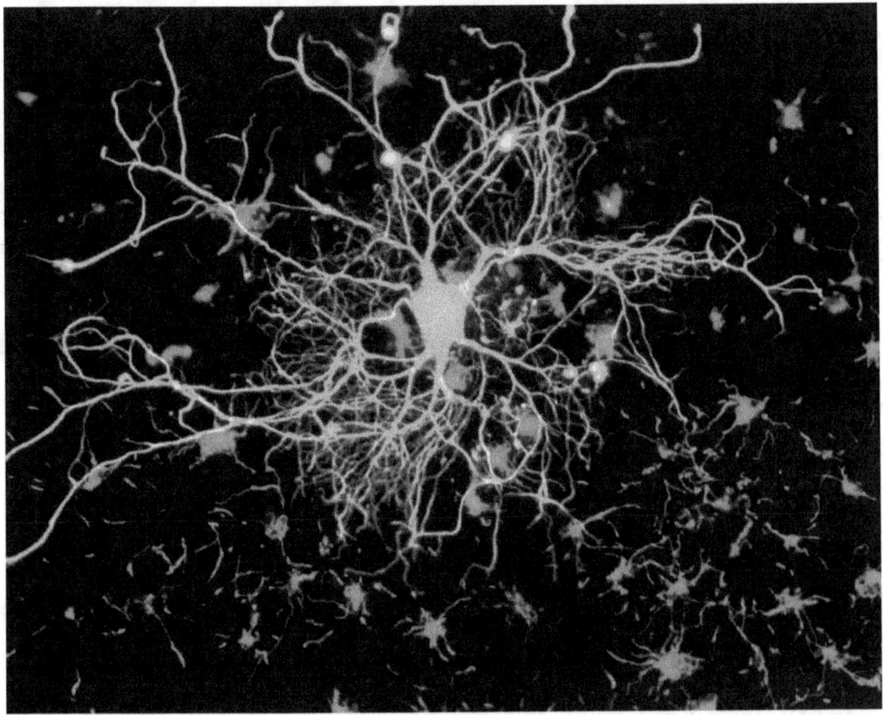

The journey of social and emotional development in childhood is a complex and dynamic process characterized by the acquisition of essential skills, the formation of relationships, and the regulation of emotions. From the tender bonds of attachment in infancy to the burgeoning friendships of early childhood, and from the emergence of empathy and moral reasoning in middle childhood to the challenges of peer interactions in adolescence, social and emotional development unfolds in a series of interconnected stages.

Attachment, the deep emotional bond between a child and their primary caregiver, lays the foundation for social and emotional development in infancy. Through sensitive and responsive caregiving, infants develop a secure base from which to explore the world, regulate their emotions, and form relationships with others. Attachment theory, pioneered by John Bowlby and Mary Ainsworth, highlights the significance of secure attachments in promoting social competence and emotional well-being throughout the lifespan.

As children transition into early childhood, they begin to engage in increasingly complex social interactions and relationships. Peer interactions become more prominent, providing opportunities for play, cooperation, and conflict resolution. Through pretend play and social games, children develop social skills such as sharing, taking turns, and perspective-taking, laying the groundwork for future friendships and peer relationships.

Middle childhood is marked by significant advances in social and emotional development, including the development of empathy, moral reasoning, and self-regulation. Children become more attuned to the feelings and perspectives of others, demonstrating increased empathy and compassion. They also begin to internalize societal norms and values, guiding their moral reasoning and decision-making processes.

Furthermore, middle childhood is a critical period for the development of peer relationships and social identity. Friendships become more stable and reciprocal, providing emotional support and companionship. Peer groups also play a crucial role in shaping children's self-concept and identity, influencing their attitudes, interests, and behaviors.

As children enter adolescence, social and emotional development takes on new dimensions as they navigate the challenges of identity formation, peer pressure, and autonomy. Adolescents grapple with questions of self-identity, seeking to establish a sense of autonomy and independence from their parents. Peer relationships become increasingly influential, shaping adolescents' attitudes, values, and behaviors.

Moreover, adolescence is a time of heightened emotional intensity, as adolescents experience fluctuations in mood, self-esteem, and self-concept. They may wrestle with issues of identity confusion, peer rejection, and social comparison, as they strive to find their place in the social world.

In summary, social and emotional development in childhood is a multi-faceted journey characterized by the acquisition of social skills, the formation of relationships, and the regulation of emotions. From the secure attachments of infancy to the complex dynamics of adolescent peer relationships, children navigate a myriad of developmental milestones and challenges that shape their social competence and emotional well-being.

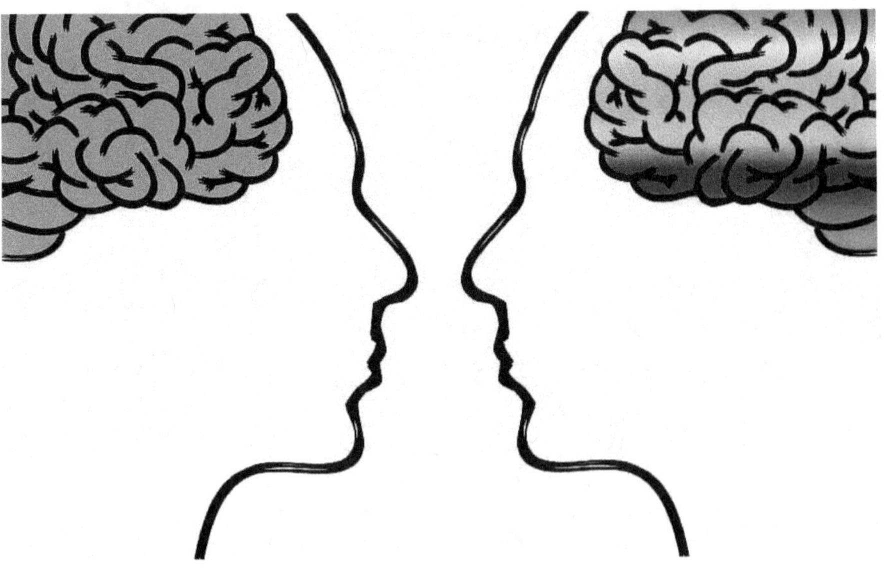

7

7

Attachment Theory and its Role in Psychological Growth

Attachment theory, proposed by John Bowlby and further developed by Mary Ainsworth, offers profound insights into the nature of human relationships and their impact on psychological growth. At its core, attachment theory posits that the quality of early relationships, particularly those with caregivers, profoundly influences individuals' emotional regulation, social competence, and overall well-being throughout life.

The foundation of attachment theory lies in the innate human need for social connection and security. From the moment of birth, infants are biologically predisposed to seek proximity to caregivers who provide comfort, protection, and nurturance. Through repeated interactions with caregivers, infants form attachment bonds that serve as a secure base from which to explore the world and regulate emotions.

Ainsworth's groundbreaking research identified three primary attachment styles: secure attachment, insecure-avoidant attachment, and insecure-anxious/ambivalent attachment. Securely attached infants exhibit a healthy balance of attachment behaviors, seeking comfort from caregivers when distressed and confidently exploring their environment. In contrast, insecurely attached infants demonstrate patterns of either avoidance or ambivalence in their interactions with caregivers, reflecting difficulties in trust, intimacy, and emotional regulation.

The quality of early attachment experiences profoundly influences individuals' socioemotional development and interpersonal relationships across the lifespan. Securely attached individuals tend to develop trusting, supportive relationships characterized by intimacy, empathy, and effective communication. They also demonstrate greater resilience in the face of stress and adversity, drawing upon their secure base to navigate life's challenges.

In contrast, individuals with insecure attachment styles may experience difficulties in forming and maintaining healthy relationships. Those with insecure-avoidant attachment may struggle with intimacy and emotional expression, while those with insecure-anxious/ambivalent attachment may exhibit clinginess, jealousy, and fear of abandonment in relationships.

Attachment theory also highlights the critical role of caregivers in fostering secure attachment bonds with their children. Responsive, sensitive caregiving promotes the development of secure attachments, providing infants with a sense of safety, trust, and emotional security. Conversely, inconsistent, neglectful, or abusive caregiving can disrupt attachment bonds, leading to insecure attachment styles and emotional difficulties.

Moreover, attachment theory emphasizes the role of internal working models, or mental representations of relationships, in shaping individuals' expectations and behaviors in relationships. Early attachment experiences influence the formation of internal working models, which guide individuals' perceptions of self, others, and relationships throughout life. These internalized representations can influence interpersonal dynamics, attachment behaviors, and coping strategies in adulthood.

In summary, attachment theory provides a powerful framework for understanding the profound impact of early relationships on psychological growth and well-being. By elucidating the dynamics of attachment bonds, internal working models, and interpersonal relationships, attachment theory offers valuable insights into the complexities of human attachment and its role in shaping individuals' developmental trajectories.

Attachment Theory and its Role in Psychological Growth

Attachment theory, formulated by John Bowlby and expanded upon by Mary Ainsworth, provides a comprehensive framework for understanding the profound impact of early relationships on psychological growth and development. At its core, attachment theory posits that infants are biologically predisposed to seek proximity to their primary caregiver, typically the mother, in times of distress or threat. Through repeated interactions with their caregiver, infants develop internal working models of relationships that shape their expectations, beliefs, and behaviors in future relationships.

The quality of early attachments plays a crucial role in shaping psychological growth across the lifespan. Ainsworth's seminal research identified three main attachment patterns: secure attachment, insecure-avoidant attachment, and insecure-ambivalent attachment. Infants with secure attachments exhibit trust, confidence, and a belief in the availability of their caregiver as a secure base from which to explore the world. In contrast, infants with insecure-avoidant attachments may avoid or ignore their caregiver, displaying minimal distress upon separation and little seeking of comfort upon reunion. Infants with insecure-ambivalent attachments may display clingy, dependent behavior, and intense distress upon separation, yet resist comfort upon reunion.

The quality of early attachments sets the stage for subsequent socioemotional development, influencing various aspects of psychological growth. Children with secure attachments tend to develop positive self-esteem, emotional regulation skills, and healthy social relationships. They are more likely to explore their environment, seek out social support, and develop adaptive coping strategies in the face of stress or adversity. Moreover, secure attachments serve as a protective factor against the development of psychopathology, buffering individuals from the negative impact of early trauma or adverse experiences.

Conversely, insecure attachments are associated with a range of socioemotional difficulties and psychological challenges. Children with insecure-avoidant attachments may struggle with intimacy, emotional expression, and trust in relationships. They may adopt defensive coping mechanisms, such as emotional distancing or denial of attachment needs, to protect themselves from rejection or disappointment. Children with insecure-ambivalent attachments may experience heightened anxiety, dependency, and difficulty regulating emotions, leading to difficulties in forming stable, satisfying relationships.

Furthermore, attachment theory highlights the lifelong implications of early attachment experiences on psychological growth and well-being. Internal working models of relationships established in infancy continue to shape individuals' expectations, beliefs, and behaviors in adulthood. Romantic relationships, friendships, and parent-child relationships are all influenced by early attachment experiences, impacting individuals' ability to trust, communicate, and form intimate connections.

In summary, attachment theory underscores the critical role of early relationships in shaping psychological growth and development. By fostering secure attachments, caregivers provide a foundation for healthy socioemotional development, resilience, and well-being across the lifespan. Understanding the profound impact of attachment experiences offers valuable insights into the complexities of human relationships and the pathways to psychological growth and flourishing.

8

8

Adolescence: Identity Formation and Challenges

Adolescence marks a pivotal period of psychological growth and exploration, characterized by the quest for identity and the navigation of numerous developmental challenges. From the onset of puberty to the transition into adulthood, adolescents grapple with questions of self-identity, autonomy, and belonging, as they seek to define who they are and where they fit in the world.

Central to adolescence is the process of identity formation, a multifaceted journey of self-discovery and exploration. Erik Erikson, a renowned developmental psychologist, described adolescence as a stage of psychosocial development marked by the conflict of identity versus role confusion. Adolescents strive to develop a coherent sense of self, integrating various aspects of their identity, including gender, ethnicity, sexuality, and interests. Identity exploration involves trying out different roles, values, and beliefs, as adolescents seek to understand themselves and their place in society.

Identity formation is influenced by a myriad of factors, including biological changes, cognitive development, social interactions, and cultural influences. Puberty, with its physical transformations and hormonal fluctuations, plays a significant role in shaping adolescents' self-concept and body image. Cognitive advances, such as abstract thinking and perspective-taking, enable adolescents to contemplate complex questions of identity and meaning, challenging conventional beliefs and values.

Moreover, social interactions and peer relationships assume heightened importance during adolescence, as adolescents seek validation, acceptance, and belonging from their peers. Peer groups serve as crucibles for identity exploration, providing opportunities for self-expression, social comparison, and the formation of shared values and norms. Adolescents may experiment with different identities, adopting various personas or subcultural affiliations, as they strive to find a sense of identity and belonging.

Despite the opportunities for self-discovery, adolescence is also a time of significant challenges and vulnerabilities. Adolescents may experience identity confusion, self-doubt, and existential angst as they grapple with the complexities of identity formation. Peer pressure, social media, and societal expectations can exacerbate feelings of inadequacy and insecurity, leading to issues such as low self-esteem, identity crisis, and risk-taking behaviors.

Furthermore, adolescence is a period of transition and upheaval, as adolescents navigate the challenges of autonomy, independence, and responsibility. Strained relationships with parents, conflicts over rules and boundaries, and the pressure to conform to peer norms can contribute to emotional turmoil and interpersonal conflicts. Adolescents may struggle to assert their autonomy while still relying on parental support and guidance, leading to tensions and power struggles within the family.

In summary, adolescence is a transformative period of identity formation and exploration, characterized by both opportunities and challenges. By navigating the complexities of self-discovery, autonomy, and social relationships, adolescents embark on a journey of growth, resilience, and self-realization. Understanding the intricacies of adolescence offers valuable insights into the developmental processes that shape individuals' identities, beliefs, and aspirations as they transition into adulthood.

Adolescence is a pivotal period of development marked by profound physical, cognitive, social, and emotional changes. Central to this transformative phase is the process of identity formation, wherein individuals grapple with questions of self-identity, values, beliefs, and aspirations. As adolescents navigate the complexities of identity development, they encounter a myriad of challenges and opportunities that shape their sense of self and their trajectories into adulthood.

Erik Erikson, a prominent developmental psychologist, proposed that adolescence is characterized by the psychosocial crisis of identity versus role confusion. During this stage, adolescents strive to establish a coherent sense of self and a sense of belonging within their social and cultural contexts. They explore different roles, identities, and value systems, seeking to reconcile their own desires and aspirations with societal expectations and norms.

Identity formation in adolescence is influenced by a multitude of factors, including individual characteristics, family dynamics, peer relationships, cultural values, and societal influences. Adolescents may draw upon various sources of identity, such as ethnicity, gender, sexuality, religion, and interests, as they construct their sense of self. They may experiment with different roles, personas, and social groups in search of a sense of belonging and authenticity.

Moreover, adolescence is a time of heightened self-awareness and self-consciousness, as individuals become acutely aware of how they are perceived by others. Social media, in particular, plays a significant role in shaping adolescents' self-image and identity construction, providing a platform for self-expression, comparison, and identity exploration.

However, the process of identity formation is not without its challenges and struggles. Adolescents may experience identity confusion, uncertainty, and identity crises as they grapple with conflicting roles, expectations, and values. They may feel pressure to conform to peer norms, societal ideals, or parental expectations, leading to identity foreclosure or a premature commitment to a particular identity or life path.

Furthermore, adolescents may face identity-related stressors such as bullying, discrimination, or identity-based prejudice, which can have profound implications for their psychological well-being and sense of belonging. Adolescents from marginalized or minority groups may experience unique challenges in navigating multiple identities and reconciling conflicting cultural expectations.

Despite these challenges, adolescence is also a time of exploration, growth, and self-discovery. Adolescents have the opportunity to explore their interests, passions, and talents, forging a sense of identity that reflects their unique strengths and aspirations. Supportive relationships with peers, family members, mentors, and role models can provide a nurturing environment for identity exploration and validation.

In summary, adolescence is a period of intense identity formation and exploration, characterized by both challenges and opportunities. By navigating the complexities of identity development, adolescents lay the groundwork for future growth, autonomy, and fulfillment. Understanding the dynamics of identity formation in adolescence offers valuable insights into the complexities of human development and the pathways to self-discovery and authenticity.

9

9

Cognitive Changes in Adolescence

Adolescence is a period of significant cognitive development, characterized by advances in reasoning, problem-solving, and abstract thinking. As adolescents transition from childhood to adulthood, they undergo profound changes in cognitive abilities, which shape their understanding of themselves, others, and the world around them.

One of the key cognitive changes that occur during adolescence is the development of formal operational thinking, as proposed by Jean Piaget. According to Piaget's theory of cognitive development, adolescents enter the formal operational stage around the age of 11 or 12, marked by the ability to think abstractly, hypothetically, and systematically. Adolescents in this stage can engage in deductive reasoning, logic, and hypothetical-deductive thinking, enabling them to consider multiple perspectives, evaluate complex problems, and engage in scientific reasoning.

Moreover, adolescence is characterized by advances in metacognition, or thinking about one's own thinking. Adolescents become more self-aware of their thoughts, beliefs, and cognitive processes, allowing them to reflect on their own reasoning, monitor their learning strategies, and adapt their problem-solving approaches accordingly. Metacognitive skills play a crucial role in academic achievement, as adolescents learn to set goals, plan tasks, and regulate their cognitive processes effectively.

Furthermore, adolescence is a period of heightened cognitive flexibility and creativity. Adolescents demonstrate an increased capacity for divergent thinking, generating multiple solutions to a given problem and thinking outside the box. They may explore novel ideas, challenge conventional wisdom, and engage in creative expression through art, music, literature, and other forms of self-expression. Cognitive flexibility allows adolescents to adapt to changing circumstances, consider alternative viewpoints, and innovate in various domains of life.

However, alongside these cognitive advances, adolescence is also a time of cognitive vulnerabilities and challenges. The development of executive functions, such as inhibitory control, working memory, and cognitive flexibility, continues throughout adolescence and into early adulthood. Adolescents may struggle with impulse control, decision-making, and planning, as they navigate the complexities of peer pressure, risk-taking, and decision-making in social contexts.

Moreover, adolescence is a period of heightened susceptibility to cognitive biases and distortions. Adolescents may exhibit egocentrism, the tendency to view the world from their own perspective and have difficulty understanding others' viewpoints. They may also engage in black-and-white thinking, or dichotomous reasoning, where issues are seen in terms of extremes with little consideration of nuance or complexity.

In summary, adolescence is a period of profound cognitive development, characterized by advances in formal operational thinking, metacognition, creativity, and cognitive flexibility. As adolescents grapple with the complexities of identity, relationships, and future goals, their cognitive abilities play a crucial role in shaping their understanding of themselves and their place in the world. Understanding the cognitive changes that occur during adolescence provides valuable insights into the challenges and opportunities inherent in this developmental stage.

Adolescence is a period of significant cognitive development, marked by profound changes in thinking abilities, problem-solving skills, and decision-making processes. As adolescents transition from childhood to adulthood, they undergo transformations in various cognitive domains, guided by both biological maturation and environmental experiences.

One of the key cognitive changes in adolescence is the development of abstract thinking and hypothetical reasoning. Adolescents become increasingly capable of thinking about ideas, concepts, and possibilities that are not directly observable. They can engage in deductive reasoning, logical analysis, and critical thinking, allowing them to explore complex ideas and formulate abstract theories about the world around them.

Furthermore, adolescents experience advancements in metacognition, or the ability to think about and reflect on their own thoughts and cognitive processes. They become more aware of their cognitive strengths and weaknesses, develop strategies for problem-solving and decision-making, and engage in self-directed learning and goal-setting. Metacognitive skills play a crucial role in academic achievement, self-regulation, and lifelong learning.

Additionally, cognitive changes in adolescence include improvements in information processing speed, working memory capacity, and attentional control. Adolescents become more efficient at processing and storing information, allowing them to handle increasingly complex tasks and academic demands. They also develop greater inhibitory control and cognitive flexibility, enabling them to adapt to changing environments and resist impulsivity.

Social and emotional factors play a significant role in shaping cognitive changes during adolescence. Peer interactions, social relationships, and cultural influences provide opportunities for cognitive growth and identity exploration. Adolescents may engage in collaborative problem-solving, perspective-taking, and peer mentoring, fostering cognitive development through social interaction and collaboration.

However, adolescence is also a period of cognitive vulnerabilities and risk-taking behavior. The rapid changes in the brain's structure and function, particularly in regions involved in decision-making and impulse control, may contribute to heightened risk-taking, sensation-seeking, and susceptibility to peer influence. Adolescents may engage in risky behaviors such as substance use, reckless driving, or delinquency, as they navigate the challenges of identity formation and peer pressure.

Moreover, cognitive changes in adolescence have implications for education, parenting, and youth development. Educators can leverage adolescents' growing cognitive abilities to promote active learning, critical thinking, and creative problem-solving in the classroom. Parents and caregivers can support adolescents' cognitive development by providing opportunities for autonomy, decision-making, and exploration, while also offering guidance and support in navigating challenges and risks.

In summary, adolescence is a period of profound cognitive changes characterized by advancements in abstract thinking, metacognition, and information processing. By understanding the cognitive dynamics of adolescence, educators, parents, and policymakers can foster environments that support cognitive growth, resilience, and positive youth development.

FIRMNESS
VENERATION
SELF ESTEEM
CONSCIENTIOUSNESS
HOPE
BENEVOLENCE
APPROBATIVENESS
CONTINUITY
SUBLIMITY
IDEALITY
SPIRITUALITY
SUAVITY
CAUTIOUSNESS
CAUSALITY
MIRTHFULNESS
INHABITIVE NESS
FRIENDSHIP
SECRETIVENESS
ACQUISITIVENESS
CONSTRUCTIVENESS
TIME
MEMORY
LOCALITY
TUNE
HISTORY
PHILOPROGENITIVENESS
CONJUGAL LOVE
COMBATIVENESS
DESTRUCTIVENESS
ALIMENTIVENESS
WEIGHT
GRAVITY
ORDER
SIZE
VITATIVENESS
CALCULATION
LANGUAGE
FORM
AMATIVENESS

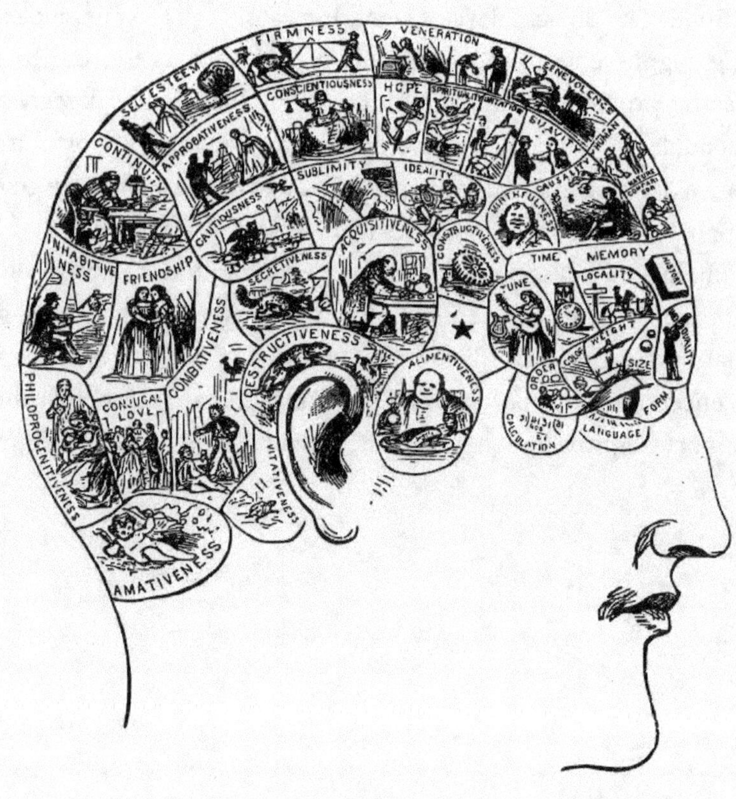

10

10

Social and Emotional Development in Adolescence

Adolescence is a time of significant social and emotional development, marked by the exploration of identity, the formation of relationships, and the navigation of complex emotions. As adolescents transition from childhood to adulthood, they grapple with a myriad of social and emotional challenges and opportunities that shape their sense of self and their interactions with others.

One of the central tasks of adolescence is the formation of a coherent and stable sense of identity. Adolescents explore different aspects of themselves, including their interests, values, beliefs, and aspirations, as they seek to answer fundamental questions about who they are and who they want to become. Identity exploration may involve experimenting with different roles, personas, and social groups, as adolescents strive to reconcile their own desires and aspirations with societal expectations and norms.

Peer relationships play a crucial role in social and emotional development during adolescence. Adolescents spend increasing amounts of time with peers, forming close friendships, and engaging in social activities that provide opportunities for companionship, support, and belonging. Peer relationships offer a platform for identity exploration, social comparison, and the development of empathy, cooperation, and conflict resolution skills.

Moreover, romantic relationships become increasingly prominent during adolescence, as individuals experience their first romantic attractions, crushes, and relationships. Romantic relationships provide opportunities for intimacy, emotional expression, and the exploration of romantic feelings and desires. They also present challenges related to communication, boundaries, and managing emotions, as adolescents navigate the complexities of love, attraction, and romantic commitment.

Emotionally, adolescence is a time of heightened intensity and variability, as individuals experience a wide range of emotions, from excitement and joy to sadness, anger, and anxiety. Adolescents may grapple with mood swings, emotional volatility, and heightened self-consciousness as they strive to understand and regulate their emotions in the face of peer pressure, academic stress, and social expectations.

Furthermore, adolescence is a period of identity-related stressors, including identity confusion, peer rejection, and identity-based prejudice or discrimination. Adolescents from marginalized or minority groups may face additional challenges in navigating multiple identities and reconciling conflicting cultural expectations. Supportive relationships with family members, mentors, and peers can provide a buffer against the negative impact of identity-related stressors, fostering resilience and positive coping strategies.

In summary, adolescence is a time of significant social and emotional development characterized by identity exploration, peer relationships, and emotional volatility. By understanding the social and emotional dynamics of adolescence, parents, educators, and policymakers can support adolescents' healthy development, resilience, and well-being as they navigate the challenges and opportunities of this transformative period.

Adolescence is a transformative period characterized by significant changes in social and emotional development. As individuals transition from childhood to adulthood, they navigate a complex array of social relationships, emotional experiences, and identity exploration that shape their sense of self and their interactions with others.

One of the key aspects of social development in adolescence is the increasing importance of peer relationships. Peers play a central role in adolescents' lives, serving as sources of support, companionship, and identity exploration. Peer groups provide opportunities for socialization, belonging, and intimacy, as adolescents navigate the complexities of friendship, peer acceptance, and peer influence.

Furthermore, adolescence is a time of heightened self-awareness and self-consciousness, as individuals become increasingly attuned to their own thoughts, feelings, and identities. Adolescents may engage in introspection, self-reflection, and identity exploration as they seek to understand who they are and where they fit in the world. This process of identity formation is influenced by a myriad of factors, including family dynamics, cultural values, and societal expectations.

Emotionally, adolescence is marked by intense and fluctuating emotions as individuals grapple with the challenges of identity exploration, peer pressure, and autonomy. Adolescents may experience heightened levels of stress, anxiety, and mood swings as they navigate the transitions and uncertainties of adolescence. Emotional regulation, the ability to manage and express emotions effectively, becomes increasingly important during this period, as adolescents learn to cope with stressors and navigate interpersonal relationships.

Moreover, adolescence is a time of exploration and experimentation with social roles, values, and behaviors. Adolescents may engage in risk-taking behaviors such as substance use, delinquency, or sexual experimentation as they seek to assert their independence and autonomy. Peer influence, media exposure, and cultural norms play significant roles in shaping adolescents' attitudes, beliefs, and behaviors, influencing their choices and decisions.

However, adolescence is also a period of opportunity for social and emotional growth, resilience, and identity consolidation. Supportive relationships with parents, peers, and mentors can provide a nurturing environment for adolescents to explore their identities, build social skills, and develop coping strategies. Positive experiences such as academic success, extracurricular involvement, and community engagement can bolster adolescents' self-esteem, confidence, and sense of purpose.

In summary, adolescence is a dynamic and transformative period characterized by significant changes in social and emotional development. By understanding the challenges and opportunities of adolescence, parents, educators, and policymakers can create supportive environments that foster positive youth development, resilience, and well-being. By navigating the complexities of adolescence with empathy, understanding, and support, adolescents can emerge stronger, more resilient, and better equipped to navigate the challenges of adulthood.

11

11

Peer Influence and Peer Relationships

During adolescence, peer relationships play a crucial role in shaping social and emotional development, identity formation, and behavior. As adolescents seek to establish independence from their families and navigate the complexities of the social world, peers become increasingly influential in their lives.

Peer influence refers to the ways in which peers can impact each other's attitudes, beliefs, values, and behaviors. Adolescents are highly susceptible to peer influence due to their desire for acceptance, belonging, and social approval. Peer groups provide a context for social comparison, identity exploration, and conformity, as adolescents seek to fit in with their peers and adhere to group norms.

One of the key mechanisms of peer influence is socialization, wherein adolescents learn social skills, cultural norms, and behavioral expectations through interactions with their peers. Peer groups serve as platforms for learning, socialization, and the transmission of cultural values, as adolescents observe, imitate, and internalize the attitudes and behaviors of their peers.

Moreover, peer influence can manifest in various forms, including peer pressure, peer modeling, and peer socialization. Peer pressure occurs when peers exert direct or indirect pressure on an individual to conform to group norms or engage in certain behaviors. Peer modeling involves observing and imitating the behaviors of peers, whether positive or negative. Peer socialization refers to the process by which peers shape each other's attitudes, values, and behaviors through interactions and shared experiences.

However, peer influence is not always negative or coercive. Positive peer relationships can promote prosocial behaviors, empathy, and cooperation, as adolescents learn to navigate conflicts, negotiate relationships, and support each other. Peer support networks provide emotional support, companionship, and validation, buffering individuals from the stresses and challenges of adolescence.

Furthermore, peer relationships evolve over the course of adolescence, becoming more complex and nuanced as individuals mature and develop. Early adolescence is characterized by the formation of cliques and peer groups based on shared interests, activities, or identities. As adolescents transition into middle and late adolescence, peer relationships become more diverse and inclusive, with individuals forming friendships based on mutual respect, trust, and intimacy.

In summary, peer influence and peer relationships play a central role in adolescent development, shaping socialization, identity formation, and behavior. By understanding the dynamics of peer influence, parents, educators, and policymakers can create supportive environments that promote positive peer relationships, resilience, and well-being. By fostering healthy peer relationships and empowering adolescents to make positive choices, we can help them navigate the challenges and opportunities of adolescence with confidence and resilience.

Peer relationships play a central role in the lives of adolescents, exerting a powerful influence on their social, emotional, and cognitive development. As individuals navigate the transition from childhood to adulthood, peers become increasingly significant sources of support, companionship, and influence. Peer relationships provide opportunities for socialization, belonging, and identity exploration, shaping adolescents' attitudes, behaviors, and sense of self in profound ways.

One of the key aspects of peer influence is its impact on adolescents' attitudes, beliefs, and behaviors. Adolescents often look to their peers for guidance, validation, and approval, seeking acceptance and belonging within their social groups. Peer influence can manifest in various forms, including peer pressure, conformity, and modeling, as adolescents adopt the attitudes and behaviors of their peers to fit in and gain acceptance.

Moreover, peer relationships serve as important contexts for social learning and skill development. Through interactions with peers, adolescents learn important social skills such as cooperation, communication, conflict resolution, and empathy. Peer relationships provide opportunities for practicing social roles, negotiating differences, and developing a sense of reciprocity and trust, essential skills for navigating interpersonal relationships throughout life.

However, peer influence is not always positive, and adolescents may also experience negative peer interactions such as peer rejection, bullying, or exclusion. Negative peer experiences can have detrimental effects on adolescents' self-esteem, mental health, and well-being, leading to feelings of loneliness, social anxiety, and depression. It is essential for parents, educators, and caregivers to be attuned to the dynamics of peer relationships and provide support and guidance to adolescents as they navigate the challenges of peer interactions.

Despite the potential challenges, peer relationships can also serve as sources of support, companionship, and resilience during adolescence. Close friendships provide emotional support, understanding, and companionship, buffering adolescents from the stresses and strains of adolescence. Peer relationships also offer opportunities for identity exploration and self-expression, as adolescents share experiences, interests, and values with their peers.

Furthermore, peer relationships play a crucial role in adolescents' social and emotional development. Adolescents learn about themselves and others through their interactions with peers, gaining insights into social norms, values, and expectations. Peer relationships provide opportunities for identity exploration, self-expression, and autonomy, as adolescents negotiate their identities within the context of their social groups.

In summary, peer influence and peer relationships are integral components of adolescent development, shaping adolescents' social, emotional, and cognitive growth in profound ways. By understanding the dynamics of peer relationships and providing support and guidance, parents, educators, and caregivers can help adolescents navigate the complexities of peer interactions and foster positive peer relationships that promote resilience, well-being, and healthy development.

MUSIC
&
PSYCHOLOGY
TALENT, SYNESTHESIA
AND THE 42 MODES
ANDER B. ESCASAIN

12

12

Family Dynamics and Psychological Growth

The family unit serves as the primary context for psychological growth and development, exerting a profound influence on individuals' social, emotional, and cognitive well-being from infancy through adulthood. Family dynamics, characterized by patterns of interaction, communication, and relationships among family members, play a central role in shaping psychological growth and fostering resilience, identity formation, and emotional well-being.

One of the key aspects of family dynamics is the quality of parent-child relationships. Secure attachment bonds between parents and children provide a foundation for healthy psychological development, fostering trust, emotional regulation, and social competence. Responsive, nurturing parenting practices promote positive self-esteem, autonomy, and secure attachment, buffering children from the negative impact of stress and adversity.

Furthermore, the family environment serves as a crucible for socialization, transmitting values, beliefs, and cultural norms that shape individuals' identities and behaviors. Family rituals, traditions, and routines provide a sense of stability, continuity, and belonging, fostering a strong sense of family identity and cohesion. Through interactions with family members, individuals learn important social skills, emotional regulation strategies, and problem-solving techniques that prepare them for navigating relationships and challenges beyond the family unit.

Moreover, family dynamics influence individuals' emotional well-being and mental health. Dysfunctional family dynamics, characterized by conflict, neglect, or abuse, can have detrimental effects on individuals' psychological well-being, leading to feelings of anxiety, depression, or low self-esteem. Adverse childhood experiences, such as parental divorce, parental substance abuse, or domestic violence, can leave lasting scars on individuals' mental health and contribute to the development of psychopathology later in life.

However, family dynamics are not static, and families have the capacity for growth, change, and adaptation over time. Family therapy and intervention programs provide opportunities for families to address underlying issues, improve communication, and strengthen relationships, fostering healthier family dynamics and promoting psychological growth and resilience.

Furthermore, the broader socio-cultural context shapes family dynamics and influences individuals' psychological growth. Socioeconomic status, cultural values, and societal norms all play a role in shaping family dynamics and parenting practices. Families from diverse cultural backgrounds may have unique patterns of interaction, communication, and socialization that influence individuals' identity development and psychological well-being.

In summary, family dynamics play a pivotal role in psychological growth and development, shaping individuals' social, emotional, and cognitive well-being from infancy through adulthood. By fostering secure attachment bonds, promoting positive parenting practices, and creating nurturing family environments, families can support the psychological growth and resilience of their members, laying the foundation for healthy relationships and well-being across the lifespan.

The family unit serves as the primary context for socialization, emotional support, and identity development, playing a crucial role in shaping individuals' psychological growth across the lifespan. From infancy to adulthood, family dynamics influence various aspects of psychological development, including attachment security, emotional regulation, interpersonal relationships, and identity formation.

Attachment theory, pioneered by John Bowlby and Mary Ainsworth, highlights the significance of early family dynamics in shaping attachment patterns and emotional well-being. Secure attachments to caregivers provide a foundation for psychological growth, fostering trust, confidence, and a sense of security that enables individuals to explore the world and form healthy relationships. Conversely, insecure attachments, characterized by inconsistent caregiving or parental unavailability, can lead to difficulties in emotion regulation, intimacy, and interpersonal relationships.

Furthermore, family dynamics influence the development of core beliefs, values, and identity formation. The family serves as a primary source of socialization, transmitting cultural norms, values, and traditions that shape individuals' sense of self and their place within society. Family roles, expectations, and communication patterns also play a crucial role in identity development, as individuals negotiate their identities within the context of their family systems.

Moreover, family dynamics impact individuals' interpersonal relationships and social functioning beyond the family unit. Patterns of communication, conflict resolution, and emotional expression learned within the family influence how individuals navigate relationships with peers, romantic partners, and colleagues throughout life. Positive family relationships characterized by warmth, support, and open communication foster adaptive social skills and resilience, while negative family dynamics such as conflict, criticism, or emotional neglect can undermine individuals' social and emotional well-being.

Family dynamics continue to shape psychological growth and development into adulthood, influencing various aspects of well-being, relationship satisfaction, and mental health. Marital relationships, parent-child dynamics, and sibling relationships all contribute to individuals' sense of belonging, emotional stability, and overall life satisfaction. Positive family relationships provide a source of social support, encouragement, and validation that promotes psychological resilience and well-being, while strained or dysfunctional family dynamics can contribute to stress, anxiety, and emotional distress.

In summary, family dynamics play a central role in psychological growth and development, shaping individuals' attachment patterns, identity formation, and interpersonal relationships. By understanding the complexities of family dynamics and providing support and resources to promote healthy family functioning, caregivers, therapists, and policymakers can create nurturing environments that foster psychological growth, resilience, and well-being across the lifespan.

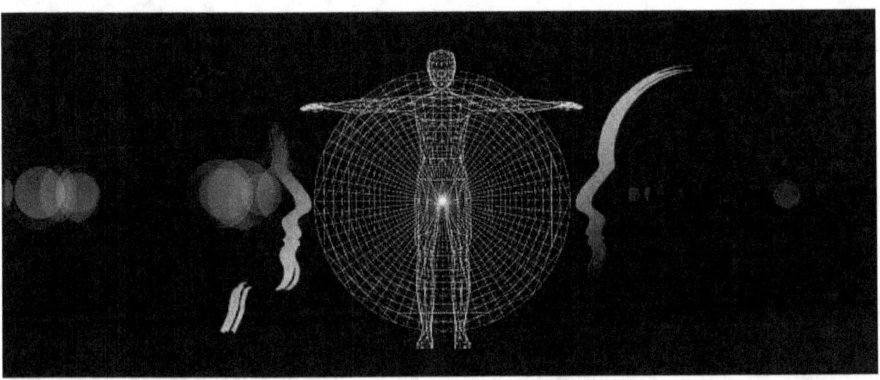

13

13

Cultural Influences on Psychological Growth

Culture exerts a profound influence on psychological growth and development, shaping individuals' beliefs, values, behaviors, and identity across the lifespan. From infancy to old age, cultural contexts provide frameworks for understanding the world, interpreting experiences, and navigating social interactions, influencing every aspect of psychological functioning.

One of the key ways culture influences psychological growth is through socialization, the process by which individuals acquire the norms, values, and behaviors of their culture. From early childhood, caregivers and community members transmit cultural beliefs and practices through language, storytelling, rituals, and social interactions. These cultural influences shape individuals' sense of self, identity, and worldview, providing a foundation for understanding their place within society.

Moreover, cultural values and norms influence various aspects of psychological development, including attachment patterns, emotion regulation, and moral reasoning. Cultural variations in caregiving practices, parenting styles, and family dynamics shape attachment relationships and emotional expression, influencing individuals' interpersonal relationships and psychological well-being. Cultural values such as collectivism or individualism shape individuals' attitudes towards relationships, autonomy, and self-expression, impacting their social and emotional development.

Furthermore, cultural contexts shape cognitive development and learning styles, influencing how individuals perceive, interpret, and process information. Cultural variations in educational practices, language use, and communication styles influence individuals' cognitive strategies, problem-solving skills, and academic achievement. Cultural beliefs about intelligence, creativity, and talent influence individuals' aspirations, motivation, and self-concept, shaping their educational and career trajectories.

Identity formation is deeply intertwined with cultural influences, as individuals negotiate their identities within the context of their cultural heritage, ethnic identity, and social group memberships. Cultural values, traditions, and rituals provide individuals with a sense of belonging and connection to their cultural communities, contributing to their sense of identity and self-esteem. Cultural identity development involves navigating complex issues of acculturation, biculturalism, and cultural adaptation, as individuals reconcile their cultural heritage with the dominant cultural norms of their society.

Moreover, cultural influences shape individuals' perceptions of mental health, help-seeking behaviors, and coping strategies. Cultural beliefs about the causes and treatment of psychological distress influence individuals' attitudes towards mental health services and their willingness to seek support. Cultural practices such as spirituality, community support networks, and traditional healing methods play important roles in promoting psychological well-being and resilience within cultural communities.

In summary, cultural influences permeate every aspect of psychological growth and development, shaping individuals' beliefs, values, behaviors, and identities from infancy to old age. By recognizing the significance of cultural contexts in shaping psychological functioning, psychologists, therapists, educators, and policymakers can promote cultural competence, inclusivity, and sensitivity in their work, fostering environments that support the psychological growth and well-being of diverse individuals and communities.

Culture serves as a powerful lens through which individuals perceive the world, interpret experiences, and navigate social interactions, exerting profound influences on psychological growth and development. From infancy to old age, cultural values, beliefs, norms, and practices shape individuals' cognitive processes, emotional experiences, identity formation, and social relationships in complex and nuanced ways.

One of the primary ways culture influences psychological growth is through its impact on socialization practices and child-rearing values. Cultural variations in parenting styles, discipline techniques, and caregiving practices shape children's attachment patterns, emotional regulation strategies, and social behaviors. For example, collectivistic cultures may emphasize inter-dependence, cooperation, and obedience to authority, while individualistic cultures may prioritize autonomy, self-expression, and assertiveness.

Moreover, cultural values and beliefs shape individuals' sense of self and identity formation. Cultural identity, the sense of belonging and connection to one's cultural heritage, plays a crucial role in shaping individuals' self-concept, values, and worldview. Cultural norms regarding gender roles, family obligations, and social expectations influence how individuals perceive themselves and their place within society, shaping their aspirations, goals, and life trajectories.

Cultural influences also extend to cognitive processes such as perception, memory, and problem-solving. Cultural schemas, or mental frameworks that organize and interpret information, influence how individuals perceive and make sense of the world. For example, cultural differences in attentional focus, categorization strategies, and memory encoding influence cognitive processes and information processing styles across cultures.

Furthermore, cultural influences shape individuals' emotional experiences, expression, and regulation strategies. Cultural norms regarding emotional display rules, coping mechanisms, and social support influence how individuals express and manage their emotions in different social contexts. For example, some cultures may encourage emotional expression and communal coping strategies, while others may emphasize emotional restraint and self-reliance.

Social relationships are also deeply influenced by cultural norms, values, and practices. Cultural variations in communication styles, interpersonal distance, and relational norms shape the dynamics of social interactions and relationships. For example, collectivistic cultures may prioritize harmony, group cohesion, and indirect communication, while individualistic cultures may prioritize autonomy, assertiveness, and direct communication.

Moreover, cultural influences on psychological growth extend beyond individual experiences to societal structures, institutions, and systems. Cultural ideologies, power dynamics, and societal norms shape access to resources, opportunities, and social mobility, influencing individuals' life chances and socio-economic outcomes.

In summary, cultural influences permeate every aspect of psychological growth and development, shaping individuals' cognition, emotion, identity, and social relationships in profound and multifaceted ways. By understanding the cultural contexts in which individuals are embedded and valuing diverse cultural perspectives, psychologists, educators, and policymakers can create more inclusive, culturally responsive approaches to promoting psychological growth, resilience, and well-being across diverse populations.

14

14

Gender Development and Identity

Gender development is a multifaceted process through which individuals come to understand and express their gender identity, roles, and behaviors. From early childhood to adulthood, individuals navigate a complex interplay of biological, social, cultural, and psychological factors that shape their sense of gender and identity.

Biologically, gender development begins with the assignment of sex at birth based on anatomical and chromosomal characteristics. However, gender identity, the internal sense of being male, female, or non-binary, is a distinct construct that may or may not align with assigned sex. Gender identity emerges gradually over time and is influenced by a combination of genetic, hormonal, and neurological factors.

Socialization plays a crucial role in shaping gender development, as individuals learn about gender roles, expectations, and stereotypes through interactions with family, peers, media, and society. From infancy, children are exposed to gendered messages and behaviors that reinforce societal norms and expectations regarding masculinity and femininity. For example, boys may be encouraged to be assertive, competitive, and independent, while girls may be encouraged to be nurturing, passive, and compliant.

Cultural influences also play a significant role in shaping gender development and identity. Cultural norms, values, and traditions regarding gender roles, sexuality, and gender expression vary widely across societies and influence how individuals understand and navigate their gender identities. For example, some cultures may have more rigid gender roles and expectations, while others may have more fluid or non-binary conceptions of gender.

Psychologically, gender development involves the internalization of gender norms and the construction of a gender identity that aligns with one's self-concept and values. Gender identity may be influenced by a combination of biological, social, and psychological factors, including individual differences in temperament, personality, and self-perception. Individuals may also experience gender dysphoria, a disconnect between their assigned sex and gender identity, which can lead to distress and discomfort.

Furthermore, gender development is influenced by interpersonal relationships and social interactions. Peers play a crucial role in shaping gender identity and expression through peer pressure, social comparison, and peer group norms. Adolescents may experiment with gender roles, expression, and identity as they seek to establish a sense of belonging and authenticity within their peer groups.

In summary, gender development and identity are complex processes influenced by a combination of biological, social, cultural, and psychological factors. By understanding the dynamics of gender development and supporting individuals' exploration and expression of their gender identities, psychologists, educators, and policymakers can create more inclusive, affirming environments that promote gender diversity, acceptance, and well-being for all individuals.

Gender development and identity formation are complex processes influenced by biological, social, cultural, and environmental factors. From early childhood to adulthood, individuals navigate the construction of gender roles, expectations, and identities, shaped by societal norms, personal experiences, and individual differences.

Biological factors, including genetic influences, hormonal profiles, and neurological differences, play a role in shaping gender development. Prenatal exposure to hormones, such as testosterone and estrogen, influences the development of physical characteristics and brain structures associated with gender identity and expression. However, it is essential to recognize that biological sex and gender identity are distinct concepts, and individuals may identify with genders that differ from their assigned sex at birth.

Socialization processes within families, peer groups, schools, and media contribute to the construction of gender roles and stereotypes. From infancy, children are exposed to gendered messages, behaviors, and expectations that shape their understanding of gender. Parents, caregivers, and educators play a significant role in reinforcing or challenging traditional gender norms through their interactions, behaviors, and attitudes toward gender expression and identity.

Peer relationships become increasingly influential in adolescence as individuals seek validation, acceptance, and belonging within their peer groups. Peer pressure, social norms, and gender-related stereotypes influence adolescents' gender identity formation and expression, shaping their attitudes, behaviors, and self-concept. Adolescents may experiment with gender roles, expressions, and identities as they navigate the complexities of peer interactions and social acceptance.

Cultural and societal norms also shape individuals' gender identities and expressions, with variations across cultures in terms of gender roles, expectations, and acceptance of diverse gender identities. Some cultures may have more rigid gender norms and expectations, while others may be more accepting of gender diversity and fluidity. Cultural traditions, religious beliefs, and historical contexts contribute to the construction of gender identities within different societies.

Furthermore, individual differences in personality, temperament, and personal experiences influence gender identity development. Some individuals may identify with binary gender categories (male or female), while others may identify with non-binary, genderqueer, or transgender identities. Gender identity is a deeply personal and subjective experience, influenced by a combination of internal factors, external influences, and individual lived experiences.

In recent years, there has been increasing recognition and acceptance of diverse gender identities and expressions, challenging traditional binary understandings of gender. Advocacy efforts, educational initiatives, and policy changes aim to promote gender inclusivity, equality, and respect for individuals of all gender identities and expressions.

In summary, gender development and identity formation are complex and multifaceted processes influenced by biological, social, cultural, and individual factors. By understanding the dynamics of gender development and promoting gender inclusivity and acceptance, society can create more supportive, equitable, and affirming environments for individuals to explore and express their gender identities authentically.

15

15

Adult Development: Challenges and Opportunities

dulthood is a dynamic and multifaceted stage of life characterized by a myriad of challenges and opportunities for growth, change, and self-discovery. As individuals navigate the complexities of adulthood, they encounter a diverse array of experiences that shape their personal and professional lives, relationships, and sense of self.

One of the key challenges of adult development is the process of managing multiple roles and responsibilities. Adults often juggle various roles, including those of spouse, parent, employee, caregiver, and community member, each demanding time, energy, and attention. Balancing these competing demands can be challenging, leading to stress, burnout, and feelings of overwhelm.

Furthermore, adulthood is often accompanied by significant life transitions and milestones, such as career changes, marriage, parenthood, and retirement. These transitions present both opportunities for growth and adaptation, as well as challenges and uncertainties. Adults may face identity crises, reevaluate their goals and priorities, and navigate changes in relationships and social roles as they transition between life stages.

Moreover, adulthood is a time of continued personal and professional development, as individuals strive to achieve their goals, fulfill their potential, and pursue meaningful endeavors. Career advancement, skill acquisition, and lifelong learning opportunities provide avenues for personal growth, fulfillment, and self-actualization. However, adults may also encounter barriers such as discrimination, economic instability, and limited access to educational and professional opportunities, hindering their ability to thrive and succeed.

In addition to external challenges, adults also grapple with internal struggles and psychological complexities. Issues such as identity exploration, existential concerns, and midlife crises are common themes in adult development. Adults may question their life choices, values, and purpose, seeking meaning and fulfillment in their personal and professional lives.

Despite these challenges, adulthood also offers numerous opportunities for personal growth, resilience, and fulfillment. Adults have the opportunity to cultivate meaningful relationships, pursue their passions, and contribute to their communities in meaningful ways. As individuals age, they often develop greater self-awareness, emotional maturity, and wisdom, allowing them to navigate life's challenges with grace and resilience.

Furthermore, adulthood provides opportunities for self-reflection, self-discovery, and personal transformation. Adults may engage in introspective practices such as therapy, mindfulness, or journaling to explore their values, beliefs, and goals. By embracing opportunities for growth and self-improvement, adults can cultivate greater fulfillment, resilience, and well-being in their lives.

In summary, adulthood is a period of both challenges and opportunities, marked by significant life transitions, personal growth, and self-discovery. By embracing life's challenges with resilience, courage, and adaptability, adults can navigate the complexities of adulthood and cultivate lives that are rich, meaningful, and fulfilling.

Adulthood is a dynamic and multifaceted stage of life characterized by a myriad of challenges and opportunities for growth, adaptation, and self-discovery. As individuals navigate the complexities of adulthood, they encounter a range of developmental tasks, transitions, and milestones that shape their personal and professional lives.

One of the primary challenges of adult development is the process of identity consolidation and self-definition. During early adulthood, individuals often grapple with questions of career choice, relationship commitments, and personal values as they strive to establish a sense of purpose and direction in life. Identity exploration and role experimentation are common during this stage, as individuals navigate the transition from adolescence to adulthood and seek to reconcile their aspirations with societal expectations and personal goals.

Moreover, adulthood is a time of significant life transitions and changes that can present both challenges and opportunities for growth. Career transitions, marriage, parenthood, and caregiving responsibilities are common life events that require adaptation, resilience, and adjustment. Balancing competing demands and responsibilities, managing work-life balance, and coping with stressors such as financial pressures, health concerns, or family obligations are ongoing challenges that individuals may face throughout adulthood.

Furthermore, interpersonal relationships and social connections play a crucial role in adult development. Building and maintaining meaningful relationships, navigating conflicts, and fostering intimacy and connection are essential tasks of adulthood. As individuals age, they may experience changes in social networks, roles, and support systems, necessitating adaptation and adjustment to evolving social dynamics.

However, adulthood also offers opportunities for personal and professional fulfillment, growth, and self-actualization. As individuals mature, they may develop greater self-awareness, emotional intelligence, and wisdom that contribute to enhanced well-being and life satisfaction. Adults may pursue new interests, hobbies, or educational opportunities, expanding their horizons and enriching their lives with new experiences and perspectives.

Moreover, adulthood is a time of continued learning, development, and self-improvement. Lifelong learning initiatives, career advancement opportunities, and personal growth pursuits enable individuals to cultivate new skills, talents, and competencies that enhance their professional success and personal fulfillment. Adult development is a journey of self-discovery and self-actualization, characterized by ongoing exploration, adaptation, and renewal.

In summary, adulthood is a dynamic and transformative stage of life characterized by a range of challenges and opportunities for growth, adaptation, and self-discovery. By navigating the complexities of adult development with resilience, optimism, and a growth mindset, individuals can harness the opportunities for personal and professional fulfillment, cultivate meaningful relationships, and lead purposeful and fulfilling lives.

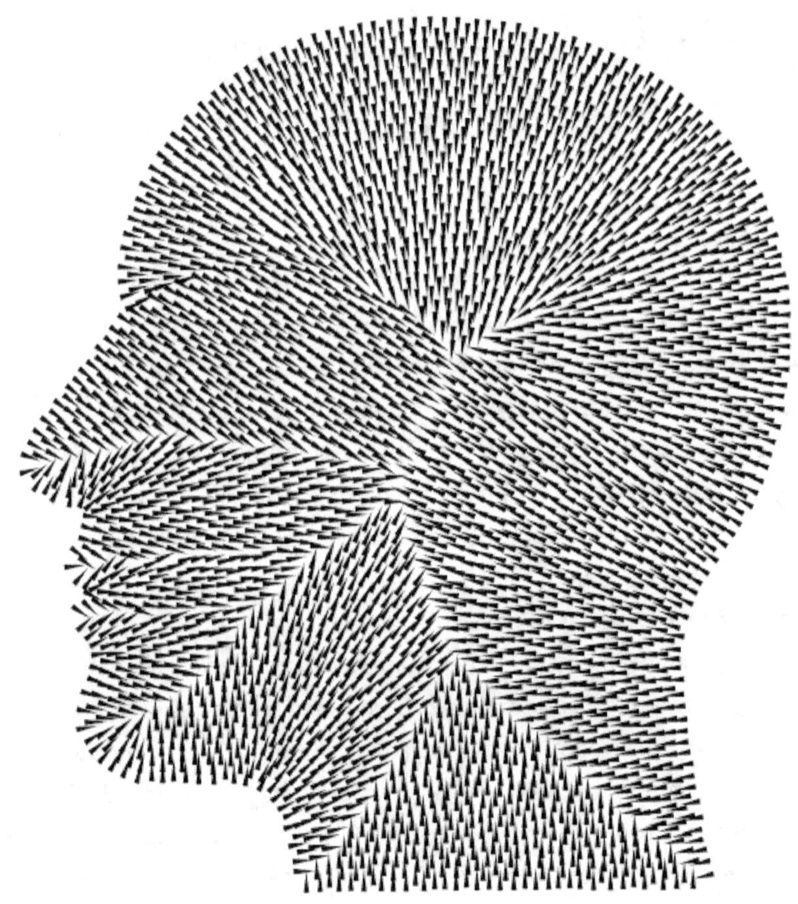

16

16

Erikson's Stages of Psychosocial Development Revisited

Erik Erikson's theory of psychosocial development outlines a series of stages that individuals progress through from infancy to old age, each characterized by a unique psychosocial crisis or challenge that must be successfully resolved for healthy development to occur. Revisiting Erikson's stages provides valuable insights into how these psychosocial challenges manifest in adulthood and their impact on individual well-being and identity formation.

The first stage, Trust vs. Mistrust, occurs during infancy and is focused on developing a sense of trust in one's caregivers and the world. In adulthood, this stage may manifest as a fundamental sense of trust in oneself, others, and the world, laying the foundation for healthy relationships and emotional well-being. Adults who have unresolved trust issues may struggle with intimacy, vulnerability, and forming meaningful connections with others.

The second stage, Autonomy vs. Shame and Doubt, occurs during early childhood and is centered around developing a sense of independence and autonomy. In adulthood, individuals revisit this stage as they strive to balance autonomy with interdependence, assertiveness with cooperation, and self-expression with consideration for others. Adults who struggle with unresolved feelings of shame and doubt may experience difficulties asserting their needs, setting boundaries, and pursuing their goals.

The third stage, Initiative vs. Guilt, occurs during the preschool years and involves developing a sense of purpose and initiative. In adulthood, individuals grapple with questions of purpose, meaning, and contribution to society. Revisiting this stage may involve reflecting on one's values, goals, and aspirations and taking proactive steps to pursue meaningful activities and relationships. Adults who struggle with unresolved guilt may experience feelings of stagnation, apathy, or self-doubt.

The fourth stage, Industry vs. Inferiority, occurs during middle childhood and focuses on developing competence and mastery in academic, social, and personal domains. In adulthood, individuals revisit this stage as they navigate career choices, skill development, and personal growth opportunities. Adults who struggle with unresolved feelings of inferiority may struggle with self-esteem, self-confidence, and a sense of accomplishment in their endeavors.

The fifth stage, Identity vs. Role Confusion, occurs during adolescence and is centered around developing a coherent sense of self and identity. In adulthood, individuals continue to explore and refine their identities, incorporating new experiences, roles, and relationships into their sense of self. Revisiting this stage may involve reconciling conflicting identities, embracing complexity, and integrating various aspects of oneself into a cohesive identity.

The sixth stage, Intimacy vs. Isolation, occurs during young adulthood and focuses on forming intimate, meaningful relationships with others. In adulthood, individuals revisit this stage as they navigate romantic relationships, friendships, and social connections. Revisiting this stage may involve developing intimacy skills, cultivating empathy and vulnerability, and fostering deep, authentic connections with others. Adults who struggle with unresolved feelings of isolation may experience loneliness, disconnection, and difficulty forming close relationships.

The seventh stage, Generativity vs. Stagnation, occurs during middle adulthood and involves contributing to society and future generations through work, parenting, mentoring, or creative endeavors. In adulthood, individuals revisit this stage as they seek to make meaningful contributions to their communities and leave a lasting legacy. Revisiting this stage may involve finding fulfillment in one's career, family life, or community involvement and finding purpose and satisfaction in giving back to others. Adults who struggle with unresolved feelings of stagnation may experience feelings of emptiness, purposelessness, or a lack of fulfillment in their lives.

The eighth stage, Integrity vs. Despair, occurs during late adulthood and involves reflecting on one's life and accepting the inevitability of mortality. In adulthood, individuals revisit this stage as they grapple with questions of meaning, legacy, and mortality. Revisiting this stage may involve finding peace, wisdom, and acceptance in the face of life's challenges and losses, and embracing the richness of one's life experiences. Adults who struggle with unresolved feelings of despair may experience regret, bitterness, or a sense of unfulfilled potential.

In summary, revisiting Erikson's stages of psychosocial development offers a valuable framework for understanding the ongoing challenges and opportunities for growth and self-discovery that individuals encounter throughout adulthood. By recognizing the psychosocial tasks inherent in each stage and addressing unresolved conflicts, individuals can navigate adulthood with resilience, authenticity, and a sense of purpose, fostering psychological well-being and personal fulfillment across the lifespan.

Erik Erikson's theory of psychosocial development outlines eight stages of human development, each characterized by a unique psychosocial crisis or challenge that individuals must navigate in order to achieve healthy development and psychological well-being. While Erikson's stages provide a valuable framework for understanding human development, it's important to revisit and reflect on these stages in light of contemporary research and societal changes.

The first stage, Trust vs. Mistrust, occurs during infancy and centers on the establishment of trust and security in the caregiver-infant relationship. Infants develop a sense of trust when their needs are consistently met with warmth and responsiveness, laying the foundation for healthy attachment relationships. Revisiting this stage highlights the importance of early bonding and attachment in shaping later psychosocial development and emphasizes the significance of nurturing caregiving practices.

The second stage, Autonomy vs. Shame and Doubt, occurs during early childhood and focuses on the development of autonomy and self-confidence. Children assert their independence and autonomy through exploration and self-expression, while caregivers provide guidance and support. Revisiting this stage underscores the importance of fostering autonomy and self-esteem in young children, while also recognizing the role of supportive caregiving in promoting healthy development.

The third stage, Initiative vs. Guilt, occurs during the preschool years and revolves around the development of initiative and a sense of purpose. Children begin to take initiative in their activities and interactions, exploring their interests and capabilities. Revisiting this stage highlights the importance of encouraging children to pursue their interests and passions, while also providing guidance and setting appropriate boundaries.

The fourth stage, Industry vs. Inferiority, occurs during middle childhood and focuses on the development of competence and mastery. Children develop a sense of industry through their achievements and accomplishments in school, sports, and other activities. Revisiting this stage emphasizes the importance of fostering a growth mindset and resilience in children, helping them navigate challenges and setbacks with perseverance and determination.

The fifth stage, Identity vs. Role Confusion, occurs during adolescence and centers on the development of identity and self-concept. Adolescents explore their values, beliefs, and goals, grappling with questions of identity and belonging. Revisiting this stage highlights the significance of providing adolescents with opportunities for self-discovery, exploration, and reflection, while also offering support and guidance as they navigate the complexities of identity formation.

The sixth stage, Intimacy vs. Isolation, occurs during young adulthood and focuses on the development of intimate relationships and connections. Young adults seek to establish meaningful relationships based on mutual trust, respect, and reciprocity. Revisiting this stage underscores the importance of fostering healthy relationships and communication skills, while also acknowledging the challenges of balancing intimacy with autonomy and independence.

The seventh stage, Generativity vs. Stagnation, occurs during middle adulthood and centers on the development of generativity and contribution to society. Adults strive to make meaningful contributions to their families, communities, and professions, leaving a lasting legacy. Revisiting this stage highlights the importance of finding purpose and fulfillment through meaningful work, relationships, and service to others.

The eighth stage, Integrity vs. Despair, occurs during late adulthood and focuses on the development of integrity and acceptance of one's life. Older adults reflect on their life experiences, achievements, and regrets, seeking to find meaning and closure. Revisiting this stage underscores the importance of promoting dignity, respect, and quality of life in older adults, while also providing support and care for those facing end-of-life issues.

In summary, revisiting Erikson's stages of psychosocial development provides valuable insights into the challenges and opportunities that individuals encounter across the lifespan. By understanding and addressing the psychosocial needs and developmental tasks associated with each stage, caregivers, educators, and policymakers can promote healthy development and psychological well being across the lifespan.

Upper Parietal Conv.
Supra-marginal Conv.
Angular Conv.
Occipital Convs.
Tempo-ral
Convs.

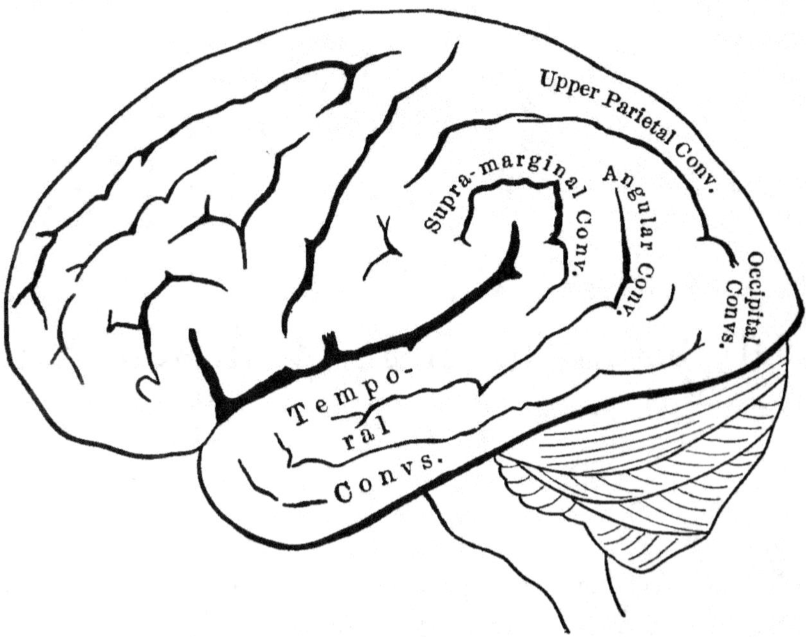

17

17

Relationships and Intimacy in Adulthood

Relationships and intimacy play fundamental roles in the lives of adults, contributing to their emotional well-being, personal growth, and overall life satisfaction. As individuals navigate the complexities of adulthood, they engage in various types of relationships, ranging from romantic partnerships to friendships, familial bonds, and professional connections, each offering unique opportunities for connection, support, and fulfillment.

Romantic partnerships are a central aspect of adult relationships, providing opportunities for emotional intimacy, companionship, and mutual support. Healthy romantic relationships are characterized by trust, respect, communication, and shared values, fostering a sense of security and belonging for individuals. Intimate partnerships offer opportunities for personal growth, self-discovery, and emotional expression, as individuals navigate the joys and challenges of building a life together.

Friendships also play a crucial role in adulthood, offering companionship, emotional support, and social connection. Friendships provide opportunities for sharing experiences, interests, and perspectives, enriching individuals' lives with laughter, companionship, and shared memories. Close friendships offer a source of comfort, understanding, and validation, helping individuals navigate the ups and downs of life with resilience and support.

Familial relationships continue to be important throughout adulthood, providing a sense of belonging, heritage, and identity. Relationships with parents, siblings, and extended family members offer opportunities for connection, tradition, and support across the lifespan. Family relationships may evolve over time, with individuals taking on new roles and responsibilities as they transition through different life stages.

Furthermore, professional relationships and networks play a significant role in adulthood, shaping individuals' career trajectories, professional development, and sense of identity. Colleagues, mentors, and professional connections offer opportunities for collaboration, mentorship, and skill development, enriching individuals' professional lives with diverse perspectives and experiences.

Intimacy in adulthood encompasses emotional, physical, and sexual aspects of relationships, fostering deeper connections and understanding between individuals. Emotional intimacy involves sharing thoughts, feelings, and vulnerabilities with a trusted partner, while physical intimacy involves affection, touch, and closeness. Sexual intimacy involves mutual desire, pleasure, and fulfillment, enhancing the bond between romantic partners.

Navigating relationships and intimacy in adulthood involves communication, empathy, and compromise, as individuals strive to meet their own needs while respecting the needs and boundaries of their partners. Effective communication skills, conflict resolution strategies, and empathy are essential for building healthy, fulfilling relationships that withstand the tests of time and adversity.

In summary, relationships and intimacy are essential aspects of adulthood, contributing to individuals' emotional well-being, personal growth, and overall life satisfaction. By cultivating healthy, supportive relationships and fostering intimacy in various aspects of their lives, adults can enhance their quality of life and experience greater fulfillment and happiness in their personal and professional relationships.

In adulthood, relationships and intimacy play essential roles in individuals' emotional well-being, personal growth, and overall quality of life. As individuals navigate the complexities of adult life, they seek connections with others that provide emotional support, companionship, and a sense of belonging. From romantic partnerships to friendships and familial bonds, relationships offer opportunities for intimacy, understanding, and mutual support.

Romantic relationships are a central aspect of adulthood, providing opportunities for intimacy, love, and companionship. As individuals form romantic partnerships, they navigate the dynamics of attraction, compatibility, and commitment. Intimate relationships require open communication, trust, and mutual respect, as partners negotiate shared goals, values, and expectations. Moreover, romantic relationships can serve as sources of personal growth, self-discovery, and emotional fulfillment, as individuals navigate challenges, conflicts, and transitions together.

Friendships also play a crucial role in adulthood, offering companionship, support, and shared experiences. Friendships provide opportunities for emotional intimacy, self-disclosure, and social connection outside of romantic relationships. Close friendships offer a sense of belonging and acceptance, as individuals share interests, values, and life experiences with trusted companions. Moreover, friendships can serve as buffers against stress, loneliness, and adversity, providing emotional support and validation during difficult times.

Familial relationships continue to be significant in adulthood, as individuals maintain connections with parents, siblings, and extended family members. Family relationships provide a sense of continuity, tradition, and identity, as individuals navigate the complexities of family dynamics and generational ties. While family relationships may evolve over time, they remain sources of emotional support, guidance, and belonging throughout adulthood.

Furthermore, intimacy in adulthood extends beyond romantic and familial relationships to include broader social connections and community involvement. Individuals seek opportunities for social engagement, belonging, and altruistic activities that foster a sense of connection and purpose. Community involvement, volunteer work, and civic engagement offer opportunities for meaningful connections with others and contribute to individuals' sense of well-being and social connectedness.

However, navigating relationships and intimacy in adulthood is not without its challenges. Individuals may encounter difficulties such as communication breakdowns, conflicts, and transitions that strain relationships and require adaptation and resilience. Balancing competing demands and responsibilities, such as work, family, and personal interests, can also pose challenges to maintaining meaningful connections with others.

Moreover, individuals may face life transitions such as marriage, parenthood, divorce, or caregiving responsibilities that impact their relationships and intimacy. These transitions require individuals to renegotiate roles, expectations, and boundaries within their relationships, fostering opportunities for personal growth, understanding, and resilience.

In summary, relationships and intimacy in adulthood are essential components of emotional well-being, personal growth, and fulfillment. By nurturing meaningful connections with others, individuals can cultivate supportive social networks, experience emotional intimacy, and find meaning and purpose in their relationships and interactions with others. By navigating the challenges and opportunities of adult relationships with empathy, understanding, and resilience, individuals can foster healthy, fulfilling relationships that contribute to their overall well-being and quality of life.

L.T.F.
R.N.F
T.
O. S.
N
N.
O. D.
T.
N.O.S.
F.C.S
N. O.D
C
F.L.D
C
T. O. D
C C.L
P.O.C.
L.
O.
F. O.
C.P
F.O.
G.A
cu
cu
L.O.S
L.O.D

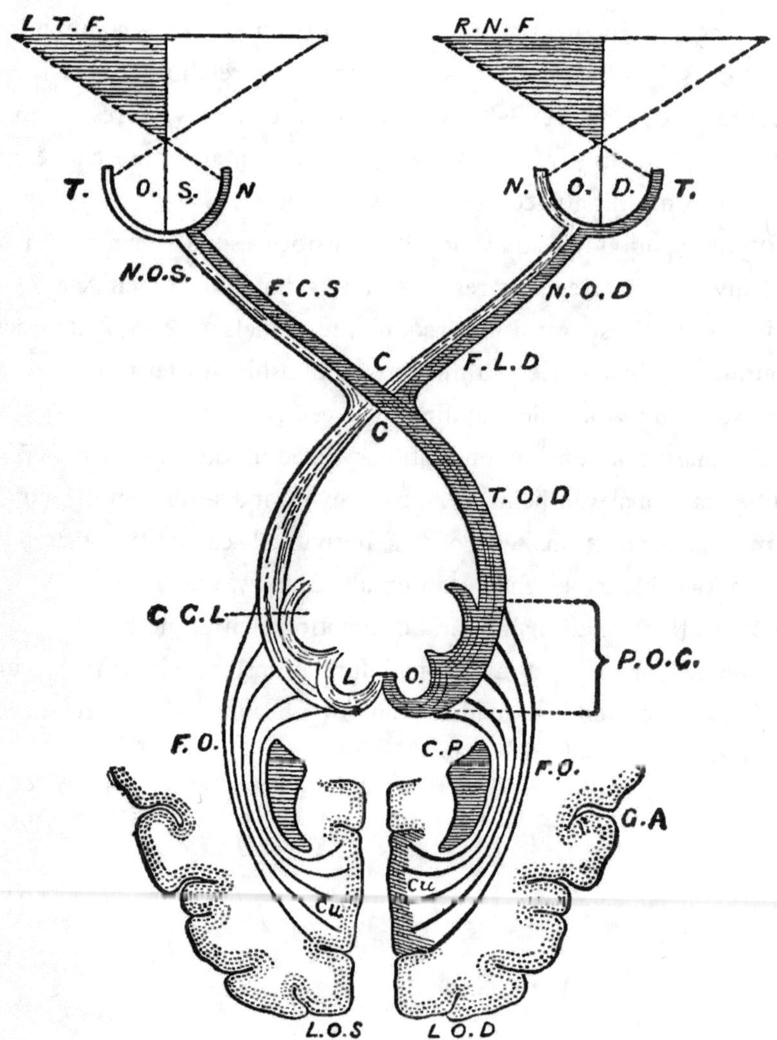

18

18

Work and Career Development

Work and career development are central aspects of adult life, influencing individuals' sense of identity, fulfillment, and financial security. From early career exploration to retirement planning, individuals navigate a series of transitions, challenges, and opportunities as they pursue meaningful and satisfying work.

Career development begins with vocational exploration during adolescence and continues throughout adulthood, as individuals explore their interests, strengths, and values and seek to align them with career opportunities. Early career decisions, such as choosing a college major or entering the workforce, set the stage for future career trajectories and development. Individuals may engage in career exploration activities such as internships, networking, and skill-building to gain insight into various industries and professions.

As individuals progress in their careers, they may experience career advancement opportunities, transitions, and changes. Career development involves continuous learning, skill development, and adaptation to changing workplace demands and opportunities. Individuals may pursue additional education, training, or certifications to enhance their skills and qualifications and increase their marketability in their chosen field.

Moreover, work and career development are influenced by various factors, including economic conditions, technological advancements, and organizational changes. Globalization, automation, and shifts in the labor market impact job availability, job security, and career pathways, necessitating flexibility and adaptability in career planning and decision-making. Individuals may need to navigate career transitions such as job loss, career changes, or re-entering the workforce after a hiatus, requiring resilience, resourcefulness, and perseverance.

Furthermore, work plays a significant role in individuals' sense of identity, self-esteem, and well-being. Meaningful work provides individuals with a sense of purpose, accomplishment, and satisfaction, contributing to their overall quality of life and psychological well-being. However, work-related stress, burnout, and dissatisfaction can have detrimental effects on individuals' mental and physical health, highlighting the importance of work-life balance, self-care, and stress management strategies.

Additionally, work and career development are influenced by cultural, social, and demographic factors. Societal expectations, gender norms, and cultural values shape individuals' career choices, opportunities, and experiences. Moreover, individuals' age, life stage, and family responsibilities influence their career decisions and priorities, as they balance work with personal and familial obligations.

In summary, work and career development are multifaceted processes that unfold over the lifespan, encompassing vocational exploration, skill development, career transitions, and personal growth. By fostering a proactive approach to career planning and development, individuals can pursue fulfilling and meaningful work that aligns with their interests, values, and aspirations. Moreover, organizations, policymakers, and educators play crucial roles in creating supportive environments that promote career development, skill-building, and work-life balance for individuals across diverse backgrounds and life stages.

Work and career development are central aspects of adulthood, shaping individuals' identities, aspirations, and overall well-being. From early career exploration to retirement planning, individuals navigate a lifelong journey of work-related experiences, challenges, and opportunities for growth and fulfillment.

Career development begins in adolescence and continues throughout adulthood, encompassing a series of stages and transitions as individuals explore, choose, and progress in their careers. During adolescence, individuals begin to explore their interests, skills, and values through academic pursuits, extracurricular activities, and part-time jobs. Career exploration during this stage involves self-assessment, researching career options, and seeking guidance from mentors, parents, and educators.

As individuals transition into young adulthood, they make important decisions regarding education, training, and career paths. This stage often involves pursuing higher education, vocational training, or entering the workforce to gain practical experience. Young adults may engage in internships, apprenticeships, or entry-level positions to explore different career options, build skills, and clarify their career goals.

During mid-career, individuals focus on advancing in their chosen professions, building expertise, and pursuing opportunities for growth and advancement. This stage often involves making strategic career decisions, such as seeking promotions, pursuing additional education or certifications, or transitioning to new roles or industries. Mid-career professionals may also face challenges such as work-life balance, burnout, or career stagnation, requiring adaptation and resilience.

In later career stages, individuals may focus on maintaining job satisfaction, preparing for retirement, and leaving a legacy. This stage involves reflecting on one's career accomplishments, values, and priorities, and making decisions regarding future career transitions or retirement plans. Older workers may seek opportunities for mentorship, knowledge transfer, or part-time work as they transition into retirement.

Moreover, work and career development are influenced by broader societal and economic factors, including technological advancements, globalization, and demographic shifts. Rapid changes in the labor market, job automation, and emerging industries require individuals to adapt, upskill, and remain agile in their careers. Additionally, diversity, equity, and inclusion initiatives aim to create more equitable and inclusive workplaces that support individuals from diverse backgrounds and identities in their career development.

Furthermore, work and career development are integral components of individuals' overall well-being and life satisfaction. Meaningful work, opportunities for growth, and a sense of purpose contribute to individuals' sense of fulfillment and psychological well-being. Conversely, job dissatisfaction, unemployment, or underemployment can negatively impact individuals' mental health, self-esteem, and overall quality of life.

In summary, work and career development are lifelong processes that shape individuals' identities, aspirations, and well-being. By engaging in ongoing career exploration, skill development, and professional growth, individuals can navigate the complexities of the modern workplace and pursue meaningful and fulfilling careers that align with their values, interests, and goals. Additionally, by fostering supportive work environments, inclusive policies, and opportunities for advancement, organizations can promote employee engagement, retention, and overall success in their career development endeavors.

19

19

Midlife Crisis or Midlife Transformation?

The notion of a "midlife crisis" has long been a cultural trope, suggesting a period of turmoil, anxiety, and dissatisfaction that individuals experience in midlife. However, contemporary perspectives challenge the idea of a midlife crisis as a universal phenomenon and instead emphasize the potential for midlife as a time of transformation, growth, and renewal.

Traditionally, the concept of a midlife crisis has been associated with feelings of discontentment, regret, and a desire for change that arise in middle adulthood, typically around the ages of 40 to 60. Individuals experiencing a midlife crisis may question their accomplishments, reevaluate their goals and priorities, and grapple with existential questions about the meaning and purpose of their lives. Common manifestations of a midlife crisis may include career changes, relationship upheavals, or impulsive behavior as individuals seek to recapture a sense of vitality and fulfillment.

However, contemporary research suggests that the midlife crisis narrative may be oversimplified and not universally experienced. Instead of viewing midlife as a period of crisis, many psychologists and researchers propose a more nuanced understanding of midlife as a time of transition, exploration, and personal growth. Rather than being driven solely by dissatisfaction or regret, midlife transitions may be fueled by a desire for self-discovery, authenticity, and meaning-making.

Midlife can be a time of reflection and introspection, prompting individuals to reassess their values, beliefs, and priorities in light of their life experiences and aspirations. This process of self-reflection may lead to significant changes in career paths, relationships, or lifestyles, as individuals seek to align their lives more closely with their authentic selves. Rather than viewing these changes as signs of crisis, they may be seen as markers of personal growth, resilience, and self-actualization.

Moreover, midlife transitions can offer opportunities for individuals to pursue new interests, passions, and goals that were previously neglected or postponed. Whether through travel, education, creative pursuits, or community involvement, midlife can be a time of exploration and reinvention, as individuals embrace new opportunities for personal fulfillment and self-expression.

Additionally, midlife transitions are not limited to negative experiences; they can also be catalyzed by positive life events such as career advancements, new relationships, or the empty nest phase of parenting. These transitions may prompt individuals to reevaluate their priorities and seize opportunities for personal and professional development, leading to a sense of empowerment, purpose, and fulfillment in midlife and beyond.

In summary, the concept of a midlife crisis is being reevaluated in contemporary psychology, with growing recognition of midlife as a period of transition, transformation, and renewal. Rather than viewing midlife transitions solely through a lens of crisis and discontentment, individuals can embrace midlife as an opportunity for self-discovery, growth, and meaningful change. By navigating midlife transitions with self-awareness, resilience, and openness to new possibilities, individuals can embark on a journey of personal transformation and fulfillment in the second half of life.

The concept of a "midlife crisis" has long been ingrained in popular culture, often portraying midlife as a period of upheaval, dissatisfaction, and existential questioning. However, contemporary research and psychological perspectives offer a more nuanced understanding of this life stage, suggesting that midlife can be a time of both challenges and opportunities for growth and transformation.

Traditionally, the midlife crisis has been described as a period of psychological turmoil and identity questioning that occurs during middle adulthood, typically around the ages of 40 to 60. Individuals experiencing a midlife crisis may exhibit symptoms such as dissatisfaction with career or relationships, feelings of restlessness or boredom, and a desire for significant life changes. This narrative often portrays midlife as a time of disillusionment and regret, where individuals grapple with the realization of unmet goals or unrealized aspirations.

However, contemporary perspectives challenge the notion of a midlife crisis as a universal experience, instead emphasizing the diversity of midlife experiences and trajectories. For many individuals, midlife represents a period of reflection, reevaluation, and personal growth—a "midlife transformation" rather than a crisis. Rather than viewing midlife challenges as inherently negative, individuals may approach this stage as an opportunity for self-discovery, renewal, and redefinition of priorities.

Midlife transformation is characterized by a reevaluation of one's values, goals, and sense of purpose, leading to meaningful changes in various areas of life. This may involve pursuing new interests or passions, making career changes, rekindling relationships, or engaging in personal development activities. Midlife can also be a time of increased self-awareness and acceptance, as individuals come to terms with their strengths, limitations, and life experiences.

Moreover, midlife can be a time of renewed vitality and creativity, as individuals draw upon their accumulated wisdom and life experiences to pursue new opportunities and challenges. Far from being a period of decline, midlife can be a time of intellectual, emotional, and spiritual growth, where individuals harness their resilience and adaptability to navigate life's transitions and uncertainties.

While midlife may present its share of challenges, such as coping with aging, health concerns, or caregiving responsibilities, it also offers opportunities for personal fulfillment, connection, and contribution to others. By embracing the process of midlife transformation, individuals can approach this stage with curiosity, openness, and resilience, recognizing it as a valuable chapter in their life journey rather than a crisis to be feared or avoided.

In summary, the concept of a midlife crisis is evolving to reflect a more nuanced understanding of midlife experiences. While challenges and transitions are inevitable, midlife can also be a time of growth, renewal, and personal transformation. By embracing the opportunities for reflection, self-discovery, and positive change that midlife offers, individuals can navigate this stage with resilience, purpose, and a sense of possibility.

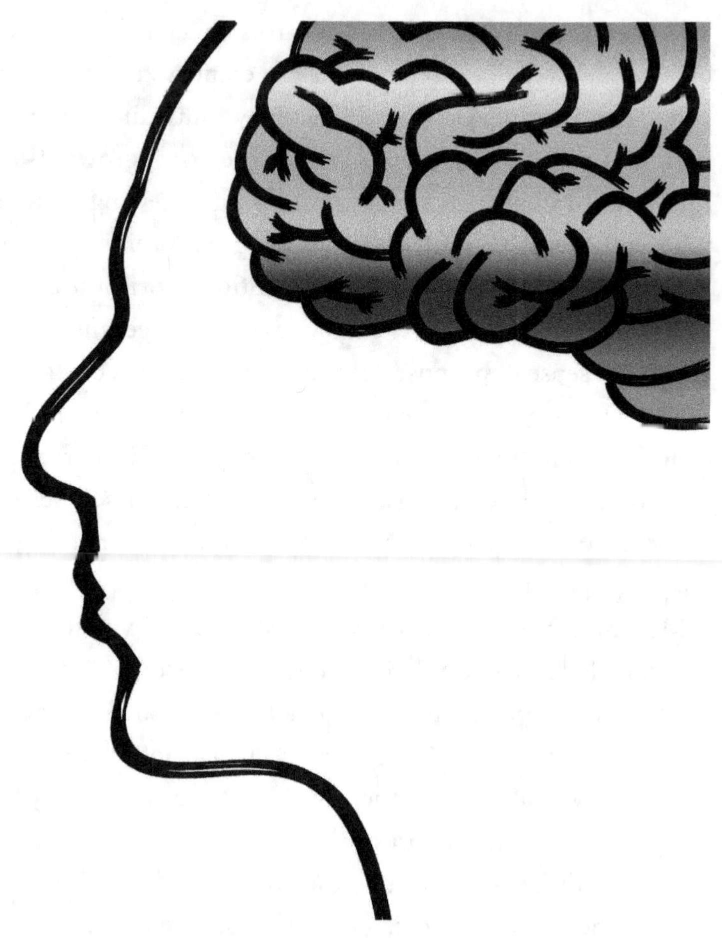

20

20

Parenting and Psychological Growth

Parenting is a profound journey of growth and transformation that shapes not only the lives of children but also the psychological development of parents themselves. From the moment a child is born, parents embark on a journey filled with joys, challenges, and opportunities for personal and relational growth.

One of the primary ways in which parenting fosters psychological growth is through the cultivation of empathy, compassion, and emotional intelligence. As parents respond to their children's needs, emotions, and behaviors, they develop a deeper understanding of themselves and others. Parenting requires empathy and attunement to children's emotions, promoting emotional awareness and regulation skills in both parents and children. Moreover, navigating the complexities of parent-child relationships fosters compassion, patience, and resilience in parents as they strive to support their children's growth and well-being.

Furthermore, parenting involves continual learning and adaptation as parents navigate the ever-changing demands and challenges of raising children. Parents learn to be flexible, creative problem-solvers, as they adapt their parenting strategies to meet their children's evolving needs and developmental stages. This process of learning and growth promotes cognitive flexibility, adaptability, and lifelong learning skills in parents, as they seek to provide the best possible environment for their children's development.

Parenting also provides opportunities for personal reflection, self-awareness, and growth. As parents grapple with their own childhood experiences, beliefs, and values, they gain insight into their own strengths, limitations, and areas for growth. Parenting challenges parents to confront unresolved issues from their past, fostering opportunities for healing, growth, and self-discovery. Moreover, the responsibilities of parenthood can inspire parents to clarify their own values, priorities, and goals, leading to personal transformation and self-actualization.

Additionally, parenting fosters the development of important relational skills, such as communication, conflict resolution, and empathy. As parents navigate the complexities of parent-child relationships, they hone their abilities to communicate effectively, set boundaries, and nurture positive connections with their children. These relational skills are not only crucial for fostering healthy parent-child relationships but also for navigating relationships in other areas of life, including romantic partnerships, friendships, and work environments.

Moreover, parenting offers opportunities for personal growth through the experience of unconditional love, joy, and fulfillment that comes from nurturing and supporting the growth of another human being. The bond between parents and children provides a source of emotional connection, meaning, and purpose that enriches parents' lives and promotes psychological well-being. Parenting challenges parents to cultivate qualities such as patience, resilience, and humility, fostering personal growth and transformation in the process.

In summary, parenting is a transformative journey that fosters psychological growth and development in both parents and children. Through the experience of parenting, individuals cultivate empathy, compassion, and emotional intelligence, while also honing their cognitive, relational, and personal growth skills. By embracing the challenges and opportunities of parenthood with openness, curiosity, and resilience, parents can experience profound personal and psychological growth that enriches their lives and the lives of their children.

Parenting is a complex and dynamic process that profoundly influences children's psychological growth and development. From infancy to adulthood, parents play a central role in shaping their children's cognitive, emotional, social, and moral development through their caregiving practices, interactions, and relationship dynamics.

During infancy, parenting behaviors such as responsiveness, warmth, and sensitivity are crucial for establishing secure attachments and fostering healthy emotional development. Secure attachment relationships provide infants with a sense of security, trust, and emotional regulation, laying the foundation for positive relationships and psychological well-being later in life. Parents who are attuned to their infants' needs, provide consistent care and affection, and respond sensitively to their cues promote healthy attachment bonds and emotional resilience.

As children grow and develop, parenting practices evolve to support their emerging autonomy, independence, and social competence. Authoritative parenting, characterized by warmth, support, and clear expectations, has been associated with positive outcomes in children, including higher self-esteem, better academic performance, and healthier social relationships. Authoritative parents provide structure and guidance while also encouraging independence, self-expression, and problem-solving skills, promoting children's psychological growth and autonomy.

Moreover, parenting styles and practices influence children's moral development and socialization into societal norms and values. Parents serve as role models for ethical behavior, empathy, and prosocial values, imparting moral principles and guiding children's moral reasoning and decision-making. By modeling kindness, empathy, and fairness in their interactions with others, parents cultivate children's empathy, moral reasoning, and social responsibility, contributing to their psychological growth and ethical development.

Parenting also plays a crucial role in shaping children's cognitive development and academic achievement. Parental involvement in children's education, including support for learning activities, communication with teachers, and encouragement of academic goals, has been linked to higher academic performance and educational attainment. Furthermore, parents who provide stimulating home environments, engage in enriching activities, and foster a love of learning contribute to children's cognitive growth, curiosity, and intellectual development.

However, parenting is not without its challenges, and parents may encounter obstacles such as stress, uncertainty, and conflicting demands that impact their ability to support their children's psychological growth. Balancing work, family, and personal responsibilities can be demanding, and parents may experience feelings of guilt, inadequacy, or burnout as they strive to meet their children's needs while also attending to their own well-being.

Despite these challenges, parenting also offers opportunities for personal growth, self-awareness, and transformation. Parenthood often prompts individuals to reflect on their own upbringing, values, and beliefs, encouraging personal growth and self-discovery. By nurturing their children's psychological growth, parents may also experience a sense of fulfillment, purpose, and connection that contributes to their own psychological well-being and satisfaction in life.

In summary, parenting is a dynamic and multifaceted process that shapes children's psychological growth and development in profound ways. By providing nurturing, supportive, and responsive caregiving, parents foster children's emotional resilience, social competence, moral development, and academic achievement. Moreover, parenting offers opportunities for personal growth, self-awareness, and fulfillment, enriching both children's and parents' lives with meaningful connections and experiences.

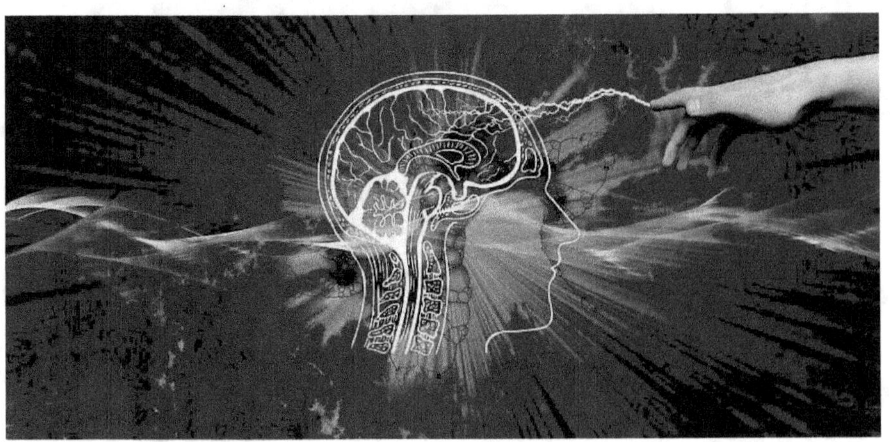

21

21

Aging and Psychological Growth

Aging is a natural and inevitable process that brings about changes in physical, cognitive, and emotional functioning. While aging is often associated with decline and loss, it also offers opportunities for psychological growth, adaptation, and resilience. As individuals navigate the later stages of life, they encounter a range of challenges and transitions that contribute to their ongoing development and well-being.

One aspect of psychological growth in aging involves the process of life review and reflection. As individuals age, they may engage in introspection, reminiscence, and evaluation of their life experiences, accomplishments, and regrets. Life review allows individuals to make sense of their past, reconcile unresolved conflicts, and find meaning and purpose in their life journey. By reflecting on their life story and personal narrative, older adults can achieve a sense of closure, acceptance, and wisdom that enhances their psychological well-being and resilience.

Moreover, aging offers opportunities for continued learning, personal growth, and self-improvement. Lifelong learning initiatives, educational programs, and creative pursuits enable older adults to pursue new interests, develop new skills, and engage in meaningful activities that promote cognitive vitality and emotional well-being. By remaining intellectually curious and socially engaged, older adults can maintain a sense of purpose, fulfillment, and connection with others throughout the aging process.

Furthermore, aging can foster emotional growth and resilience as individuals navigate the challenges of later life, such as health concerns, loss of loved ones, and changes in social roles and relationships. Older adults may develop coping strategies, emotional regulation skills, and adaptive responses to stressors that promote psychological well-being and resilience. By drawing upon their life experiences, wisdom, and coping resources, older adults can navigate life's challenges with resilience, optimism, and grace.

Additionally, aging provides opportunities for interpersonal growth and connection with others. As individuals age, they may prioritize relationships with family, friends, and community members, seeking opportunities for companionship, support, and shared experiences. Meaningful social connections and support networks contribute to older adults' emotional well-being, sense of belonging, and quality of life. By fostering meaningful relationships and social engagement, older adults can maintain a sense of connection and purpose that enriches their later years.

However, aging is not without its challenges, and older adults may encounter obstacles such as health concerns, caregiving responsibilities, and social isolation that impact their psychological well-being and quality of life. Health promotion initiatives, community support services, and age-friendly policies can help address these challenges and promote older adults' psychological growth, resilience, and well-being.

In summary, aging is a multifaceted process that offers opportunities for psychological growth, adaptation, and resilience. By engaging in life review, lifelong learning, and meaningful social connections, older adults can cultivate resilience, wisdom, and emotional well-being that enrich their later years. By recognizing and embracing the opportunities for growth and fulfillment that aging offers, individuals can navigate the aging process with resilience, grace, and a sense of purpose.

Aging is a natural and inevitable process characterized by physical, cognitive, emotional, and social changes that unfold over the lifespan. While aging is often associated with decline and loss, it also offers opportunities for psychological growth, wisdom, and resilience that contribute to overall well-being and life satisfaction.

One aspect of psychological growth in aging involves the development of wisdom—a deep understanding of life, oneself, and others, combined with an ability to apply this knowledge to navigate life's challenges effectively. Wisdom encompasses qualities such as emotional regulation, empathy, compassion, and perspective-taking, which mature with age and life experience. Older adults may draw upon their accumulated wisdom to cope with adversity, make meaningful life choices, and foster harmonious relationships with others.

Moreover, aging is often accompanied by a shift in priorities and values, as individuals reflect on their life experiences and consider what truly matters to them. Older adults may place greater emphasis on relationships, personal fulfillment, and experiences rather than material possessions or career achievements. This reprioritization of values can lead to greater contentment, satisfaction, and psychological well-being in later life.

Furthermore, aging provides opportunities for personal growth and self-discovery as individuals navigate transitions, challenges, and opportunities associated with later life stages. Retirement, for example, offers newfound freedom and flexibility for older adults to pursue hobbies, interests, and passions that may have been neglected during their working years. Volunteering, lifelong learning, and creative pursuits can foster a sense of purpose, fulfillment, and continued personal growth in retirement.

Additionally, aging can foster resilience and adaptation as individuals confront age-related changes, health challenges, and losses. Resilience—the ability to bounce back from setbacks, cope with adversity, and maintain a sense of hope and optimism—becomes increasingly important in later life. Older adults may draw upon their resilience and coping skills to navigate transitions such as widowhood, chronic illness, or changes in mobility, finding strength and meaning in the face of adversity.

Furthermore, aging is often accompanied by a greater appreciation for the present moment and a sense of gratitude for life's blessings. Older adults may savor simple pleasures, cultivate mindfulness practices, and cherish moments of connection with loved ones, finding joy and fulfillment in everyday experiences. This sense of gratitude and mindfulness can contribute to greater psychological well-being and resilience in later life.

In summary, aging offers opportunities for psychological growth, wisdom, and resilience that contribute to overall well-being and life satisfaction. By embracing the opportunities for personal growth, reflection, and adaptation that come with aging, individuals can cultivate a sense of fulfillment, meaning, and resilience in later life. Moreover, by challenging ageist stereotypes and fostering inclusive attitudes toward aging, society can promote the psychological growth and well-being of older adults, recognizing the valuable contributions and wisdom they offer to individuals and communities alike.

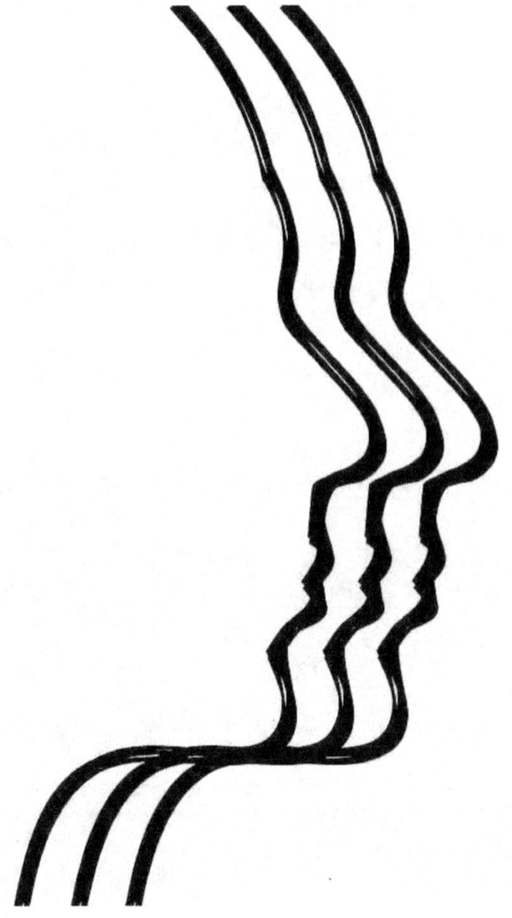

22

22

Coping with Loss and Grief

Loss is an inevitable part of the human experience, and grieving is a natural response to loss. Whether it's the death of a loved one, the end of a relationship, a major life transition, or the loss of a cherished dream, coping with loss and grief involves navigating a complex and deeply personal journey of emotional healing and adjustment.

One of the first steps in coping with loss is acknowledging and allowing oneself to experience the full range of emotions associated with grief, including sadness, anger, guilt, confusion, and numbness. It's important to recognize that grief is a natural and necessary process of mourning the significance of what has been lost and adjusting to life without it.

Additionally, seeking support from others can be instrumental in coping with loss and grief. Whether it's friends, family members, support groups, or mental health professionals, having a supportive network of people who can offer empathy, validation, and companionship can provide comfort and solace during difficult times. Sharing one's feelings and memories with others can also help individuals feel less alone in their grief and validate the significance of their loss.

Moreover, finding healthy ways to express and process emotions is essential in coping with loss and grief. This may involve journaling, art therapy, physical activity, or mindfulness practices that allow individuals to channel their emotions in constructive and meaningful ways. Engaging in self-care activities such as getting enough sleep, eating nourishing foods, and engaging in activities that bring joy and comfort can also help individuals manage the physical and emotional toll of grief.

Additionally, finding meaning and purpose in the midst of loss can be a powerful coping mechanism. This may involve finding ways to honor and memorialize the person or thing that has been lost, such as creating a memory book, participating in rituals or ceremonies, or establishing a charitable foundation in their honor. Finding ways to integrate the loss into one's life story and identity can help individuals find a sense of continuity and meaning in the face of profound loss.

Furthermore, coping with loss and grief often involves navigating the process of adjusting to a new reality and finding a sense of acceptance and peace. This may involve letting go of unrealistic expectations or fantasies about how things should have been and instead focusing on accepting the reality of what is. Acceptance does not mean forgetting or minimizing the significance of the loss but rather finding a way to integrate it into one's life story and move forward with resilience and hope.

It's important to recognize that coping with loss and grief is a highly individual and nonlinear process, and there is no "right" or "wrong" way to grieve. Each person's experience of grief is unique, and individuals may move through the stages of grief at their own pace and in their own way. By allowing oneself to feel and express emotions, seeking support from others, finding healthy coping strategies, and finding meaning and acceptance in the midst of loss, individuals can navigate the journey of grief with resilience, grace, and healing.

Loss is an inevitable part of the human experience, and grieving is a natural response to the loss of someone or something significant in our lives. Whether it's the death of a loved one, the end of a relationship, or the loss of a job, grieving is a complex and deeply personal process that involves emotional, cognitive, physical, and spiritual dimensions. Coping with loss and grief requires time, patience, and self-compassion as individuals navigate the various stages and emotions associated with grief.

One of the first stages of grief is often shock and denial, where individuals may struggle to accept the reality of the loss. This initial phase may be characterized by feelings of numbness, disbelief, and emotional detachment as individuals try to come to terms with the loss. It's important to allow oneself to experience these feelings without judgment or self-criticism, recognizing that they are a normal part of the grieving process.

As the shock wears off, individuals may experience intense emotions such as sadness, anger, guilt, or anxiety. These emotions may come in waves, fluctuating in intensity and duration over time. It's important to acknowledge and express these feelings in healthy ways, whether through talking with supportive friends or family members, journaling, or engaging in creative outlets such as art or music. Avoiding or suppressing emotions can prolong the grieving process and lead to complications such as depression or anxiety.

During the grieving process, individuals may also experience physical symptoms such as fatigue, insomnia, changes in appetite, or physical aches and pains. These symptoms are a natural response to the stress and emotional upheaval of grief and should be addressed with self-care practices such as adequate rest, nutrition, exercise, and relaxation techniques. Seeking medical attention if physical symptoms persist or worsen is also important to ensure overall well-being.

Another aspect of coping with loss and grief is finding meaning and purpose in the midst of pain and suffering. This may involve seeking support from religious or spiritual beliefs, engaging in rituals or ceremonies to honor the memory of the deceased, or finding ways to carry on the legacy of the person or thing that was lost. Connecting with others who have experienced similar losses can also provide validation, understanding, and a sense of solidarity in grief.

Furthermore, coping with loss and grief involves adjusting to life without the presence of the person or thing that was lost. This may involve making practical changes, such as reorganizing living spaces or financial matters, as well as emotional adjustments to new roles, identities, or routines. It's important to give oneself permission to grieve at one's own pace and to seek support from others when needed.

In summary, coping with loss and grief is a deeply personal and transformative process that involves acknowledging and expressing emotions, finding meaning and purpose, and adjusting to life changes. By allowing oneself to grieve in healthy ways, seeking support from others, and practicing self-care, individuals can navigate the grieving process with resilience, compassion, and hope for the future.

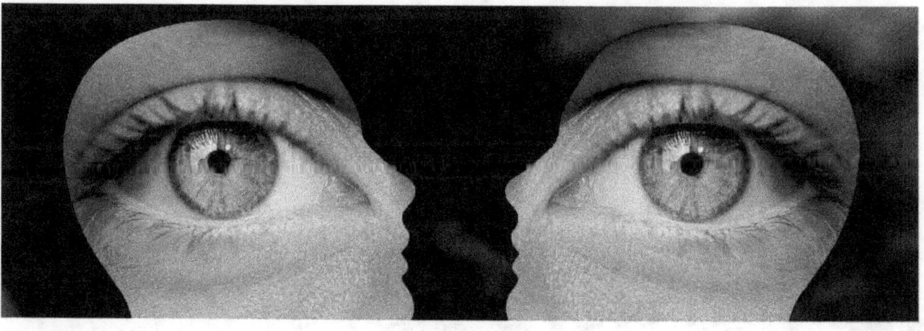

23

23

Resilience and Psychological Growth

Resilience is the capacity to bounce back from adversity, adapt to change, and thrive in the face of challenges. It involves drawing upon inner strengths, resources, and coping strategies to overcome obstacles and build psychological well-being. While adversity and setbacks are inevitable parts of life, resilience enables individuals to navigate difficult circumstances with courage, optimism, and perseverance, fostering psychological growth and transformation in the process.

One aspect of resilience is the ability to reframe adversity as an opportunity for growth and learning. Rather than viewing challenges as insurmountable obstacles, resilient individuals approach adversity with a growth mindset, recognizing the potential for personal development, self-discovery, and mastery. Adversity can serve as a catalyst for resilience, prompting individuals to tap into their inner resources, develop new skills, and cultivate resilience-building habits such as problem-solving, goal-setting, and seeking social support.

Moreover, resilience involves cultivating adaptive coping strategies that promote emotional regulation, stress management, and self-care. Resilient individuals are able to regulate their emotions effectively, acknowledging and expressing feelings such as sadness, anger, or anxiety in healthy ways. They also engage in self-care practices such as mindfulness, exercise, and relaxation techniques to manage stress and maintain a sense of balance and well-being amidst adversity.

Furthermore, resilience is fostered through social support networks and interpersonal connections that provide encouragement, validation, and practical assistance during difficult times. Resilient individuals have strong social support systems that offer emotional support, guidance, and companionship, helping them navigate adversity with greater ease and resilience. Building and maintaining supportive relationships is essential for resilience, as connections with others provide a sense of belonging, purpose, and connectedness that buffers against the impact of stress and adversity.

Another aspect of resilience is the ability to maintain a sense of optimism, hope, and gratitude in the face of adversity. Resilient individuals adopt a positive outlook on life, focusing on their strengths, accomplishments, and blessings rather than dwelling on setbacks or failures. They cultivate gratitude for the present moment and maintain hope for the future, believing in their ability to overcome challenges and create positive change in their lives.

Furthermore, resilience involves fostering a sense of meaning and purpose in life, even in the midst of suffering or hardship. Resilient individuals draw upon their values, beliefs, and sense of identity to find meaning in adversity, viewing challenges as opportunities for personal growth, contribution, and fulfillment. By aligning their actions with their core values and aspirations, resilient individuals derive a sense of purpose and direction that sustains them through difficult times and fosters psychological growth and resilience.

In summary, resilience is a dynamic and multidimensional process that enables individuals to thrive in the face of adversity and cultivate psychological growth and well-being. By adopting a growth mindset, cultivating adaptive coping strategies, building supportive relationships, maintaining optimism and hope, and finding meaning and purpose in adversity, individuals can develop resilience that fosters psychological growth, transformation, and flourishing in all aspects of life.

Resilience is the capacity to bounce back from adversity, adapt to challenges, and thrive in the face of adversity. It involves a combination of personal characteristics, coping strategies, and support systems that enable individuals to navigate difficult circumstances and emerge stronger and more resourceful.

Resilience is not about avoiding or denying adversity but rather about facing it head-on, learning from it, and using it as an opportunity for growth and transformation.

One aspect of resilience is the ability to maintain a positive outlook and mindset in the face of adversity. Optimism, hope, and a belief in one's ability to overcome challenges are key components of resilience. By reframing setbacks as temporary and solvable, individuals can cultivate a sense of agency and empowerment that enables them to persevere in the face of adversity.

Furthermore, resilience involves effective coping strategies and problem-solving skills that enable individuals to manage stress, regulate emotions, and maintain a sense of balance and well-being. Healthy coping mechanisms such as seeking social support, practicing mindfulness or relaxation techniques, and engaging in activities that bring joy and fulfillment can help individuals navigate difficult times and build resilience.

Moreover, resilience is fostered by supportive relationships and social networks that provide emotional validation, encouragement, and practical assistance during times of need. Trusted friends, family members, or mentors who offer empathy, understanding, and guidance can bolster individuals' resilience and help them navigate adversity with greater ease and confidence.

Additionally, resilience is cultivated through experiences of adversity and hardship that challenge individuals to grow, adapt, and develop new skills and perspectives. These "growth opportunities" may arise from setbacks, failures, or traumas that force individuals to reassess their priorities, values, and goals, leading to personal growth and transformation.

Moreover, resilience is not a fixed trait but rather a dynamic process that evolves over time and can be strengthened through intentional effort and practice. Building resilience involves cultivating self-awareness, self-compassion, and self-efficacy—the belief in one's ability to overcome challenges and achieve goals. By developing resilience, individuals can enhance their psychological well-being, increase their capacity to cope with stress, and thrive in the face of adversity.

In summary, resilience is a vital resource that enables individuals to navigate life's challenges and adversities with courage, strength, and adaptability. By cultivating resilience through positive mindset, effective coping strategies, supportive relationships, and growth-oriented perspectives, individuals can harness the power of adversity to foster psychological growth, personal development, and overall well-being.

Cortical
Centres for the Extremities
For the Face.
Capsula int.
Pes Pedunculi cerebii
A
Pons
C
B
Nucl fac.
N.fascialis
Pyramis
N. spinal

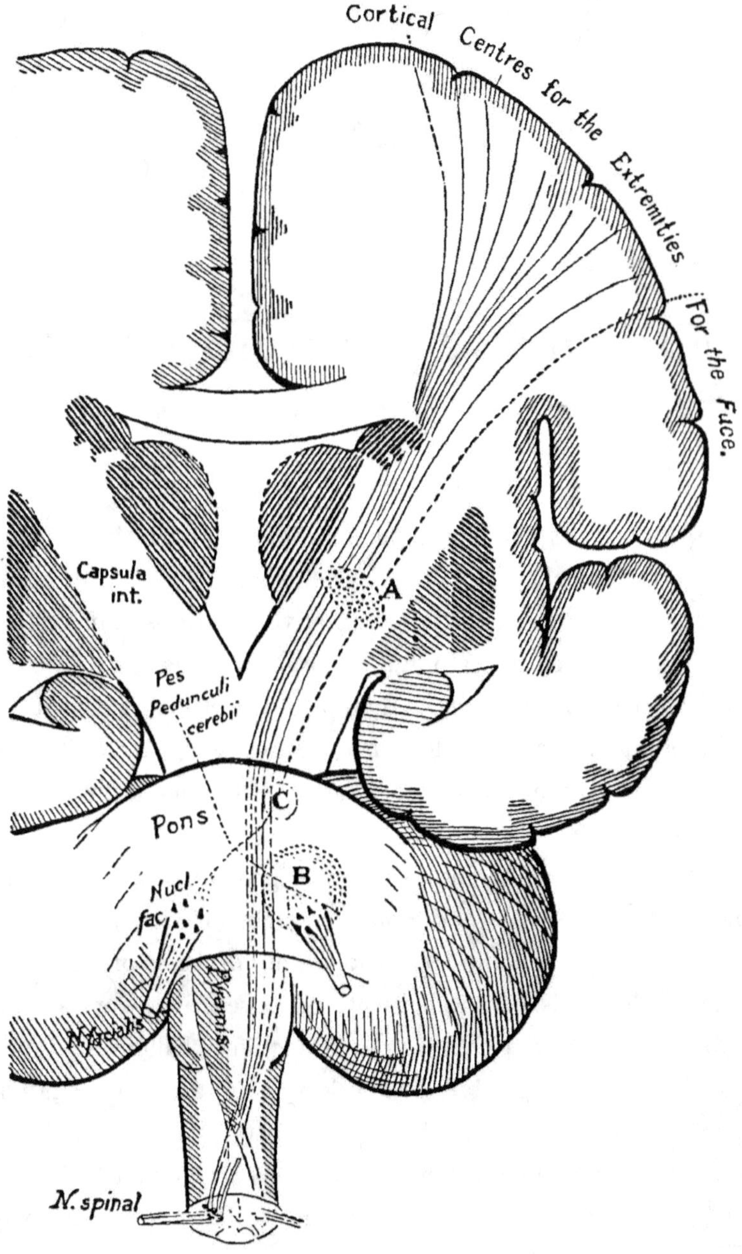

24

24

Mindfulness and Personal Growth

Mindfulness is the practice of intentionally paying attention to the present moment with openness, curiosity, and acceptance. Rooted in ancient contemplative traditions, mindfulness has gained increasing recognition in modern psychology as a powerful tool for personal growth, self-discovery, and emotional well-being. By cultivating mindfulness, individuals can deepen their awareness of their thoughts, emotions, and sensations, fostering greater self-understanding, resilience, and personal growth.

One way mindfulness promotes personal growth is by enhancing self-awareness—the ability to observe one's thoughts, feelings, and behaviors without judgment or attachment. Through mindfulness practices such as meditation, individuals learn to cultivate a non-reactive awareness of their inner experiences, allowing them to respond to life's challenges with greater clarity, insight, and perspective. By developing self-awareness, individuals can identify and challenge unhelpful thought patterns, emotional reactions, and habitual behaviors that may hinder personal growth and well-being.

Moreover, mindfulness fosters emotional regulation—the ability to recognize and manage one's emotions effectively. By practicing mindfulness, individuals learn to observe their emotions with acceptance and compassion, rather than becoming overwhelmed or reactive. Mindfulness techniques such as mindful breathing or body scanning can help individuals regulate their emotional responses, reduce stress, and cultivate a sense of calm and equanimity in the face of difficult emotions. By developing emotional regulation skills, individuals can navigate life's ups and downs with greater resilience, balance, and emotional well-being.

Furthermore, mindfulness promotes acceptance—the willingness to acknowledge and embrace one's experiences, both pleasant and unpleasant, without resistance or avoidance. By practicing acceptance, individuals learn to cultivate a non-judgmental attitude toward their thoughts, feelings, and sensations, allowing them to be present with whatever arises in the moment. This attitude of acceptance fosters greater peace of mind, self-compassion, and authenticity, enabling individuals to live more fully and authentically in alignment with their values and aspirations.

Additionally, mindfulness enhances interpersonal relationships by fostering empathy, compassion, and presence in interactions with others. By cultivating mindfulness, individuals develop the capacity to listen deeply, communicate effectively, and empathize with others' experiences and perspectives. Mindful communication promotes greater understanding, connection, and intimacy in relationships, leading to enhanced mutual respect, trust, and support. By bringing mindfulness into their relationships, individuals can cultivate deeper connections, resolve conflicts more skillfully, and foster greater harmony and well-being in their social networks.

In summary, mindfulness is a powerful practice for personal growth, self-discovery, and emotional well-being. By cultivating mindfulness, individuals can deepen their self-awareness, regulate their emotions, cultivate acceptance, and enhance their interpersonal relationships. Through regular practice and integration into daily life, mindfulness can become a transformative tool for fostering greater resilience, compassion, and fulfillment in every aspect of life.

Mindfulness is the practice of intentionally paying attention to the present moment with openness, curiosity, and acceptance. It involves cultivating awareness of one's thoughts, feelings, bodily sensations, and surroundings without judgment or attachment. Mindfulness practices, such as meditation, breathwork, and mindful movement, have been shown to promote personal growth and development in various aspects of life.

One way mindfulness facilitates personal growth is by enhancing self-awareness and insight into one's thoughts, emotions, and behaviors. By observing the patterns of the mind without getting caught up in them, individuals gain a deeper understanding of their internal experiences and habitual reactions. This increased self-awareness enables individuals to recognize unhelpful thought patterns, emotional triggers, and behavior patterns that may be holding them back from reaching their full potential.

Moreover, mindfulness fosters emotional regulation and resilience in the face of stress, adversity, and uncertainty. By learning to stay present with difficult emotions without reacting impulsively or getting overwhelmed, individuals develop greater emotional flexibility and resilience. Mindfulness practices teach individuals to cultivate a compassionate and non-judgmental attitude toward themselves and their experiences, which promotes emotional healing and well-being.

Furthermore, mindfulness cultivates a sense of presence and connection in relationships, enhancing communication, empathy, and intimacy. By practicing mindful listening and nonverbal communication, individuals can deepen their understanding and connection with others, fostering healthier and more fulfilling relationships. Mindfulness also promotes empathy and compassion toward others' suffering, leading to greater kindness, generosity, and prosocial behavior.

Additionally, mindfulness promotes cognitive flexibility and creativity by helping individuals break free from rigid thinking patterns and open themselves up to new possibilities. By cultivating a beginner's mind—a mindset of curiosity, openness, and receptivity—individuals become more open to new experiences, perspectives, and ideas. This openness to novelty and uncertainty fosters creativity, innovation, and adaptability in various domains of life.

Moreover, mindfulness practices cultivate a sense of presence and appreciation for life's simple pleasures, leading to greater overall well-being and life satisfaction. By savoring the present moment and cultivating gratitude for what is, individuals can experience greater contentment, joy, and fulfillment in their daily lives. Mindfulness also promotes a sense of purpose and meaning by helping individuals align their actions with their values and aspirations, fostering a sense of fulfillment and personal growth.

In summary, mindfulness is a powerful tool for personal growth and development, fostering self-awareness, emotional regulation, resilience, and interpersonal connection. By cultivating mindfulness practices in daily life, individuals can enhance their well-being, cultivate positive relationships, and navigate life's challenges with greater ease and grace. Mindfulness offers a pathway to personal growth and transformation, enabling individuals to live more fully and authentically in the present moment.

25

25

Self-Concept and Self-Esteem Across the Lifespan

Self-concept refers to the collection of beliefs, perceptions, and evaluations that individuals hold about themselves, including their identity, abilities, values, and roles. Self-esteem, on the other hand, reflects individuals' overall subjective evaluation of their worth and value as a person. Both self-concept and self-esteem play crucial roles in shaping individuals' thoughts, feelings, behaviors, and overall well-being across the lifespan.

During childhood, self-concept and self-esteem begin to form through interactions with caregivers, peers, and the environment. Children develop an understanding of themselves based on feedback from others, experiences of success and failure, and comparisons with peers. As children grow and develop, their self-concept becomes more complex and differentiated, encompassing various aspects of their identity, such as gender, ethnicity, interests, and abilities. Early experiences of acceptance, encouragement, and support from caregivers and peers contribute to the development of positive self-esteem, whereas experiences of rejection, criticism, or neglect may undermine self-esteem and self-worth.

During adolescence, self-concept and self-esteem undergo significant changes and challenges as individuals navigate the transition from childhood

104

to adulthood. Adolescents grapple with questions of identity, belonging, and self-discovery as they explore different roles, relationships, and identities. Peer relationships become increasingly influential in shaping adolescents' self-concept and self-esteem, as they seek validation, acceptance, and social status within their peer groups. Adolescents may experience fluctuations in self-esteem as they navigate the complexities of identity formation, social comparison, and peer pressure.

In adulthood, self-concept and self-esteem continue to evolve and adapt in response to life experiences, roles, and responsibilities. Adults may experience shifts in self-concept and self-esteem as they transition through various life stages, such as entering the workforce, starting a family, or pursuing personal goals and aspirations. Positive experiences of competence, achievement, and success can bolster self-esteem and reinforce a positive self-concept, whereas setbacks, failures, or interpersonal conflicts may challenge individuals' sense of self-worth and identity.

Moreover, self-concept and self-esteem play crucial roles in shaping individuals' mental health, emotional well-being, and overall quality of life across the lifespan. Individuals with high self-esteem tend to experience greater psychological well-being, resilience, and life satisfaction, whereas individuals with low self-esteem may be more vulnerable to depression, anxiety, and relationship difficulties. Cultivating a positive self-concept and healthy self-esteem involves fostering self-acceptance, self-compassion, and self-respect, as well as seeking support from others and engaging in activities that promote personal growth and fulfillment.

In summary, self-concept and self-esteem are dynamic and multifaceted constructs that evolve across the lifespan in response to internal and external influences. By nurturing positive self-concept and healthy self-esteem through supportive relationships, self-reflection, and self-care practices, individuals can cultivate greater resilience, well-being, and fulfillment in their lives.

Self-concept refers to the perceptions, beliefs, and attitudes individuals hold about themselves, encompassing various aspects such as identity, abilities, values, and roles. Self-esteem, on the other hand, refers to the subjective evaluation of one's worth, value, and adequacy, influencing how individuals feel about themselves and their capabilities. Both self-concept and self-esteem evolve and develop across the lifespan, influenced by internal and external factors, experiences, and social interactions.

During early childhood, self-concept and self-esteem are primarily shaped by interactions with caregivers, peers, and the environment. Children begin to form perceptions of themselves based on feedback from others, such as praise, criticism, and comparisons with peers. Positive experiences and supportive relationships contribute to the development of a positive self-concept and self-esteem, while negative experiences or lack of validation can undermine confidence and self-worth.

As children enter adolescence, self-concept and self-esteem become more complex as individuals grapple with questions of identity, belonging, and self-acceptance. Adolescents may explore different roles, identities, and peer groups as they seek to establish a sense of self and autonomy. Social comparison and peer influence play significant roles in shaping adolescents' self-concept and self-esteem, as they navigate the pressures of conformity, popularity, and societal expectations.

During adulthood, self-concept and self-esteem continue to evolve as individuals experience various life transitions, roles, and responsibilities. Career achievements, relationships, and personal accomplishments contribute to feelings of competence, success, and self-worth. However, adulthood also brings challenges such as work-related stress, relationship conflicts, and societal pressures that can impact self-esteem and self-concept.

In later adulthood, self-concept and self-esteem may be influenced by factors such as retirement, health changes, and reflections on life achievements and regrets. Older adults may experience shifts in self-perception and priorities as they adapt to changes in physical abilities, social roles, and relationships. Maintaining a positive self-concept and self-esteem in later life may involve finding meaning and purpose in activities such as volunteering, lifelong learning, and maintaining social connections.

Throughout the lifespan, individuals' self-concept and self-esteem are influenced by internal factors such as personality traits, cognitive abilities, and coping styles, as well as external factors such as cultural norms, societal expectations, and life experiences. Moreover, supportive relationships, positive feedback, and validation from others play a crucial role in fostering healthy self-concept and self-esteem across the lifespan.

In summary, self-concept and self-esteem are dynamic constructs that evolve and develop across the lifespan, influenced by internal and external factors, experiences, and social interactions. By nurturing supportive relationships, fostering self-awareness, and promoting self-acceptance, individuals can cultivate healthy self-concept and self-esteem at every stage of life, contributing to overall well-being and life satisfaction.

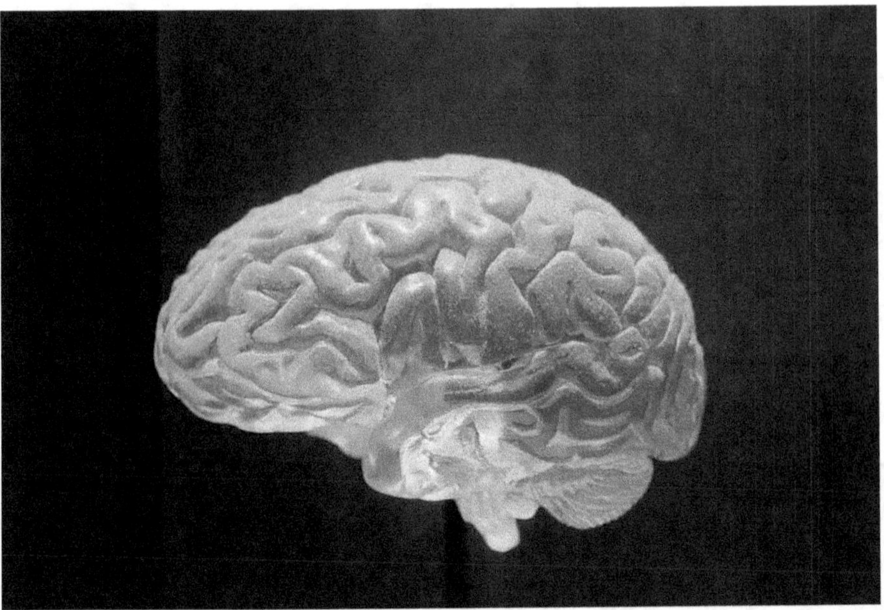

26

<h1 style="text-align:center">26</h1>

Personality Development

Personality development refers to the gradual and enduring pattern of thoughts, feelings, and behaviors that shape an individual's unique identity and character over time. Personality is influenced by a combination of genetic predispositions, environmental factors, life experiences, and social interactions, resulting in a complex and multifaceted construct that continues to evolve throughout the lifespan.

The study of personality development is rooted in various theoretical perspectives, each offering insights into the factors and processes that contribute to the formation and evolution of personality traits. One influential perspective is the psychodynamic approach, which emphasizes the role of unconscious drives, conflicts, and early childhood experiences in shaping personality development. According to Freud's psychoanalytic theory, personality is structured into three components—the id, ego, and superego—that interact dynamically to shape behavior and influence psychological functioning.

Another prominent theoretical perspective is the trait approach, which focuses on identifying and measuring consistent patterns of behavior, thoughts, and emotions that characterize individuals' personalities. Trait theories propose that personality can be described in terms of a set of enduring traits or dimensions, such as extraversion, neuroticism, agreeableness, conscientiousness, and openness to experience. These traits are thought to be relatively stable across different situations and over time, although they may be influenced by life experiences and environmental factors.

Additionally, the social-cognitive perspective emphasizes the reciprocal interaction between individuals' personalities, cognitive processes, and social environments. According to Bandura's social-cognitive theory, personality development is influenced by observational learning, social modeling, and self-efficacy beliefs—the belief in one's ability to succeed in specific situations or accomplish tasks. Individuals learn new behaviors and develop personality traits through observation, imitation, and reinforcement of social behaviors and role models.

Furthermore, the humanistic perspective emphasizes the inherent capacity for self-awareness, personal growth, and self-actualization within individuals. Humanistic theories such as Maslow's hierarchy of needs and Rogers' person-centered approach highlight the importance of fulfilling psychological needs, self-expression, and self-fulfillment in promoting healthy personality development. According to these theories, individuals strive to realize their full potential and pursue meaningful goals that align with their values and aspirations.

Personality development unfolds through various stages and transitions across the lifespan, influenced by biological, psychological, and social factors. During childhood and adolescence, individuals undergo significant developmental milestones and identity formation processes that shape their sense of self, social relationships, and worldview. Early experiences with caregivers, peers, and the environment play a crucial role in laying the foundation for personality development, influencing attachment styles, self-esteem, and coping strategies.

In adulthood, personality development continues as individuals navigate life transitions, career choices, and relationship dynamics. Personal and professional experiences, such as marriage, parenthood, career advancement, and loss, contribute to the shaping of personality traits, values, and priorities. Moreover, individuals may engage in self-reflection, self-discovery, and personal growth activities that promote greater self-awareness, authenticity, and fulfillment.

In later adulthood, personality development may be characterized by reflection on life achievements, legacy, and existential concerns. Older adults may undergo personality changes in response to retirement, health changes, or loss of loved ones, leading to shifts in priorities, values, and attitudes. Despite the potential for age-related changes, personality traits tend to show stability over time, with some evidence suggesting that certain traits may even increase or decrease in intensity as individuals age.

In summary, personality development is a complex and multifaceted process that unfolds across the lifespan, shaped by genetic, environmental, and social factors. By understanding the underlying mechanisms and influences on personality development, individuals can gain insight into their own personality traits, motivations, and behaviors, fostering self-awareness, personal growth, and well-being.

Personality development refers to the gradual and enduring pattern of thoughts, feelings, and behaviors that characterize an individual over time. It encompasses the unique combination of traits, attitudes, values, and behavioral tendencies that shape how individuals perceive themselves, interact with others, and navigate the world around them. Personality development is influenced by a complex interplay of genetic, biological, psychological, and environmental factors, unfolding across the lifespan through various stages and transitions.

During infancy and early childhood, personality development is primarily shaped by genetics, temperament, and early experiences with caregivers. Infants begin to display distinct temperamental traits such as activity level, adaptability, and emotional reactivity, laying the foundation for later personality development. Parenting styles, attachment relationships, and environmental factors such as socioeconomic status and cultural norms also influence early personality development.

As children grow and develop, their personalities become more complex and differentiated, influenced by cognitive, social, and emotional factors. The preschool years mark the emergence of self-awareness, social skills, and moral development, as children begin to understand themselves in relation to others and develop a sense of right and wrong. Peer relationships, school experiences, and exposure to diverse environments further shape children's personality development, fostering traits such as empathy, resilience, and curiosity.

During adolescence, personality development is characterized by identity exploration, self-discovery, and autonomy-seeking. Adolescents grapple with questions of identity, values, and goals as they strive to establish a sense of self and independence. Peer influence, societal expectations, and cultural norms play significant roles in shaping adolescents' self-concept and identity, influencing their attitudes, behaviors, and aspirations.

In adulthood, personality development continues to evolve as individuals navigate various life roles, relationships, and responsibilities. Career choices, intimate relationships, and life experiences contribute to the development of personality traits such as conscientiousness, agreeableness, and openness to experience. Moreover, personality may undergo changes in response to major life events such as marriage, parenthood, career transitions, or trauma, reflecting individuals' capacity for adaptation and growth.

In later adulthood, personality development may be influenced by factors such as retirement, health changes, and reflections on life achievements and regrets. Older adults may experience shifts in personality traits such as openness, agreeableness, and emotional stability as they adapt to changes in physical abilities, social roles, and relationships. Despite the potential for personality stability, research suggests that personality traits may continue to evolve and develop throughout the lifespan, reflecting individuals' ongoing growth and adaptation to life circumstances.

In summary, personality development is a lifelong process characterized by continuity, change, and adaptation to internal and external influences. By understanding the complex interplay of genetic, biological, psychological, and environmental factors that shape personality, individuals can cultivate self-awareness, resilience, and personal growth, contributing to their overall well-being and life satisfaction.

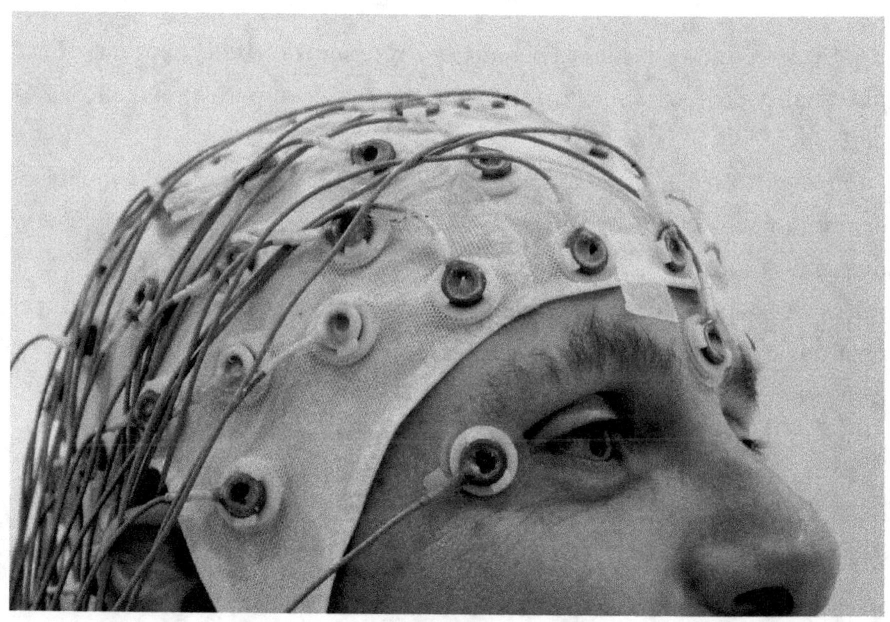

27

27

Positive Psychology and Well-Being

Positive psychology is a branch of psychology that focuses on studying and promoting factors that contribute to human flourishing, happiness, and well-being. It emphasizes the importance of understanding and cultivating strengths, positive emotions, resilience, and meaningful connections in order to lead fulfilling and satisfying lives. Positive psychology seeks to complement traditional approaches to psychology, which have often focused more on pathology and dysfunction, by highlighting the importance of fostering positive experiences and outcomes.

One key concept within positive psychology is subjective well-being, which refers to individuals' overall evaluations of their lives, including their experiences of happiness, satisfaction, and fulfillment. Subjective well-being encompasses both cognitive evaluations of life satisfaction and affective experiences of positive emotions such as joy, gratitude, and contentment. Positive psychology research examines factors that contribute to subjective well-being, such as positive relationships, engagement in meaningful activities, and a sense of purpose or meaning in life.

Moreover, positive psychology emphasizes the importance of cultivating strengths and virtues that contribute to resilience and psychological well-being. This approach focuses on identifying and leveraging individuals' inherent strengths, talents, and virtues, such as kindness, curiosity, perseverance, and gratitude, to promote personal growth and flourishing. By developing and using their strengths, individuals can enhance their resilience, cope more effectively with adversity, and experience greater satisfaction and fulfillment in life.

Another key aspect of positive psychology is the study of positive emotions and their role in promoting well-being. Positive emotions such as joy, love, gratitude, and awe not only feel good but also have important psychological and physiological benefits. Research has shown that experiencing positive emotions can broaden individuals' attention and cognitive resources, enhance creativity and problem-solving abilities, and build psychological resilience. Positive psychology interventions, such as gratitude exercises, acts of kindness, and mindfulness practices, aim to cultivate positive emotions and promote well-being.

Furthermore, positive psychology emphasizes the importance of fostering positive relationships and social connections as fundamental aspects of well-being. Strong social support networks, meaningful connections with others, and a sense of belonging are essential for promoting psychological resilience, happiness, and overall life satisfaction. Positive psychology interventions often involve activities that promote social connection, such as collaborative projects, group activities, and community engagement initiatives.

In summary, positive psychology offers a holistic approach to understanding and promoting well-being by focusing on strengths, positive emotions, meaningful connections, and a sense of purpose in life. By cultivating strengths, fostering positive emotions, nurturing social connections, and finding meaning in life, individuals can enhance their overall well-being and lead more fulfilling and satisfying lives. Positive psychology interventions provide practical tools and strategies for promoting well-being and resilience, empowering individuals to thrive and flourish in all aspects of their lives.

Positive psychology is a branch of psychology that focuses on the study of human strengths, virtues, and optimal functioning, with the aim of promoting well-being and enhancing quality of life. Unlike traditional psychology, which often focused on pathology and dysfunction, positive psychology emphasizes the cultivation of positive emotions, strengths, and virtues that contribute to individuals' flourishing and fulfillment.

One key aspect of positive psychology is the study of positive emotions, such as happiness, gratitude, joy, and contentment, and their impact on overall well-being. Research has shown that experiencing positive emotions not only enhances subjective well-being but also promotes physical health, resilience, and coping abilities. Positive psychology interventions, such as gratitude journaling, acts of kindness, and savoring positive experiences, have been shown to increase happiness and life satisfaction.

Moreover, positive psychology emphasizes the importance of identifying and utilizing one's strengths and virtues to enhance well-being and achieve personal goals. Character strengths such as kindness, resilience, creativity, and perseverance play a central role in individuals' ability to thrive and flourish in various aspects of life. By recognizing and leveraging their unique strengths, individuals can enhance their self-esteem, confidence, and sense of purpose, leading to greater overall well-being.

Positive psychology also emphasizes the cultivation of meaningful relationships and social connections as essential components of well-being. Strong social support networks, nurturing relationships, and a sense of belonging contribute to individuals' happiness, resilience, and overall life satisfaction. Positive psychology interventions aimed at improving interpersonal relationships, communication skills, and empathy can enhance social connectedness and foster a sense of community and belonging.

Furthermore, positive psychology emphasizes the importance of finding meaning and purpose in life as a key driver of well-being and fulfillment. Individuals who have a clear sense of purpose, goals, and values tend to experience greater satisfaction and meaning in their lives, even in the face of adversity. Positive psychology interventions such as goal-setting, values clarification, and finding meaning in difficult experiences can enhance individuals' sense of purpose and existential well-being.

In summary, positive psychology offers a holistic approach to promoting well-being and enhancing quality of life by focusing on the cultivation of positive emotions, strengths, relationships, and meaning in life. By integrating principles and practices from positive psychology into everyday life, individuals can cultivate resilience, happiness, and fulfillment, leading to a more meaningful and satisfying life journey. Positive psychology reminds us that well-being is not just the absence of distress but also the presence of positive emotions, engagement, relationships, meaning, and accomplishment.

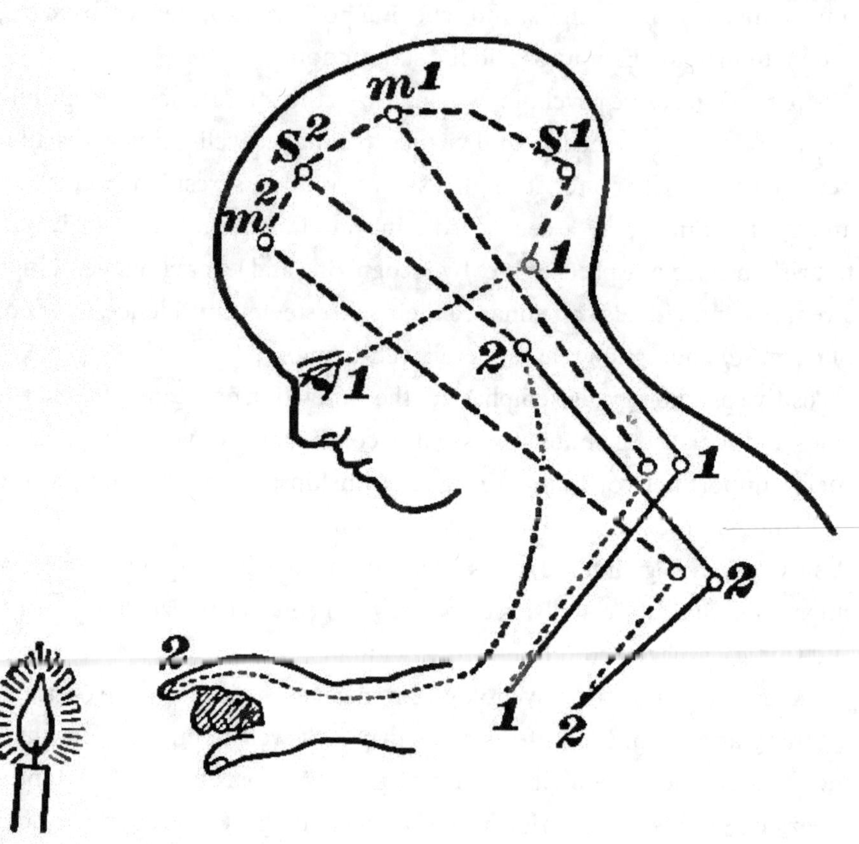

28

28

Creativity and Innovation: Psychological Perspectives

reativity and innovation are fundamental to human progress, driving advancements in science, technology, arts, and culture. From groundbreaking inventions to artistic masterpieces, creativity and innovation shape the way we live, work, and interact with the world around us. Psychological perspectives offer valuable insights into the processes, factors, and conditions that foster creativity and innovation.

One key aspect of creativity is divergent thinking—the ability to generate a variety of novel and original ideas or solutions to a problem. Psychological research has identified several cognitive processes and strategies that contribute to divergent thinking, including associative thinking, flexible thinking, and the ability to overcome mental blocks or fixedness. Creative individuals often exhibit traits such as openness to experience, curiosity, and a willingness to take risks, which enable them to explore unconventional ideas and perspectives.

Moreover, creativity is influenced by both intrinsic and extrinsic factors, including motivation, environment, and social context. Intrinsic motivation, driven by a genuine interest or passion for the task at hand, fosters creativity by encouraging individuals to engage in activities for their own sake rather than external rewards. Extrinsic factors such as supportive environments, collaboration, and feedback also play important roles in nurturing creativity by providing resources, encouragement, and opportunities for growth.

Furthermore, creativity often involves a process of incubation, where ideas are allowed to percolate and develop over time. This incubation period may involve periods of intense focus and concentration, followed by periods of relaxation or distraction, during which the unconscious mind continues to work on the problem. Psychological research suggests that taking breaks, engaging in unrelated activities, or exposing oneself to new experiences can facilitate the incubation process and lead to creative insights and breakthroughs.

Innovation, on the other hand, involves the application of creative ideas or solutions to address real-world problems or challenges. While creativity is the generation of novel ideas, innovation is the implementation of those ideas to create value or effect change. Psychological perspectives on innovation emphasize the importance of collaboration, risk-taking, and resilience in the innovation process.

Collaboration and interdisciplinary teamwork are often essential for bringing creative ideas to fruition and overcoming barriers to innovation. By pooling diverse perspectives, expertise, and resources, teams can generate more innovative solutions and address complex problems more effectively. Moreover, fostering a culture of psychological safety, where individuals feel comfortable taking risks, sharing ideas, and challenging the status quo, is crucial for promoting innovation within organizations and society.

Additionally, resilience plays a vital role in the innovation process, as setbacks, failures, and uncertainty are inevitable when pursuing innovative endeavors. Psychologically resilient individuals and organizations are better equipped to adapt to setbacks, learn from failure, and persevere in the face of adversity. By embracing a growth mindset, reframing challenges as opportunities for learning and growth, and maintaining a sense of optimism and determination, innovators can overcome obstacles and bring their creative visions to fruition.

In summary, creativity and innovation are multifaceted processes influenced by cognitive, motivational, social, and environmental factors.

Psychological perspectives offer valuable insights into the mechanisms and conditions that foster creativity and innovation, from cognitive processes such as divergent thinking to motivational factors such as intrinsic motivation and collaboration. By understanding and applying these psychological principles, individuals, teams, and organizations can cultivate creativity and drive innovation to address pressing challenges and create positive change in the world.

Creativity and innovation are fundamental aspects of human cognition and behavior, driving progress, discovery, and adaptation in various domains of life. From artistic expression to scientific breakthroughs, creativity and innovation play crucial roles in problem-solving, adaptation to new challenges, and the advancement of society. Psychological research offers insights into the cognitive, emotional, and social processes underlying creativity and innovation, shedding light on how individuals generate novel ideas, overcome obstacles, and bring about change.

One key psychological perspective on creativity emphasizes the role of cognitive processes such as divergent thinking, associative thinking, and flexible problem-solving in generating novel ideas and solutions. Divergent thinking involves generating multiple potential solutions to a problem, breaking free from conventional or linear thinking patterns to explore new possibilities. Associative thinking involves making connections between seemingly unrelated ideas or concepts, fostering creativity through the synthesis of diverse perspectives and knowledge domains. Flexible problem-solving involves approaching challenges with an open mind, willingness to experiment, and willingness to tolerate ambiguity, allowing individuals to overcome obstacles and generate innovative solutions.

Moreover, psychological research suggests that creativity is influenced by various individual and environmental factors, including personality traits, cognitive abilities, motivation, and social context. Certain personality traits, such as openness to experience, curiosity, and tolerance for ambiguity, have been linked to higher levels of creativity. Cognitive abilities such as fluency, flexibility, and originality also play important roles in creative thinking and problem-solving. Additionally, intrinsic motivation, autonomy, and a supportive environment that encourages risk-taking and experimentation can foster creativity and innovation.

Furthermore, emotions and affective states such as curiosity, fascination, and flow have been found to enhance creativity by promoting cognitive flexibility, motivation, and engagement in creative activities. Positive emotions such as joy and excitement can enhance cognitive flexibility and associative thinking, while negative emotions such as frustration or anxiety may hinder creativity by narrowing attention and inhibiting exploration. The state of flow, characterized by intense focus, immersion, and enjoyment in a task, has been associated with heightened creativity and innovation, as individuals experience a sense of effortless engagement and heightened awareness.

From a social perspective, creativity and innovation often emerge through collaborative processes, social networks, and cultural influences that foster idea exchange, feedback, and collaboration. Interdisciplinary collaboration, diversity of perspectives, and exposure to different cultural norms and values can stimulate creativity by challenging assumptions, fostering cross-pollination of ideas, and promoting innovation through collective intelligence. Moreover, supportive social networks, mentorship, and recognition of creative achievements play crucial roles in nurturing individuals' creative potential and facilitating the dissemination of innovative ideas.

In summary, creativity and innovation are multifaceted phenomena that involve cognitive, emotional, and social processes operating at individual, interpersonal, and societal levels. By understanding the psychological mechanisms underlying creativity and innovation, individuals, organizations, and societies can foster environments that stimulate creative thinking, promote collaboration, and harness the transformative power of human imagination to address complex challenges and shape a better future.

Creativity and innovation are essential drivers of human progress, fueling advancements in science, technology, art, and culture. Psychological research offers valuable insights into the cognitive, emotional, and environmental factors that influence creative thinking and innovative problem-solving. By understanding these psychological perspectives, individuals and organizations can foster creativity and innovation to tackle complex challenges and inspire positive change.

One psychological perspective on creativity emphasizes the role of divergent thinking—the ability to generate multiple, novel solutions to a problem—as a key component of creative thinking. Divergent thinking involves breaking free from conventional ideas and exploring alternative perspectives, leading to innovative insights and breakthroughs. Psychological research suggests that individuals who engage in divergent thinking tend to have flexible cognitive processes, high levels of curiosity, and a willingness to take risks, all of which facilitate creative problem-solving.

Moreover, creativity is influenced by various cognitive processes, including associative thinking, pattern recognition, and analogical reasoning. Associative thinking involves making connections between seemingly unrelated ideas or concepts, leading to novel combinations and insights. Pattern recognition allows individuals to discern meaningful patterns or relationships in information, leading to creative solutions or discoveries. Analogical reasoning involves drawing parallels between disparate domains or situations, facilitating innovative problem-solving by applying insights from one context to another.

Furthermore, creativity is influenced by intrinsic motivation—the desire to engage in creative activities for their own sake, rather than external rewards or incentives. Intrinsic motivation fosters a sense of autonomy, mastery, and purpose, enabling individuals to pursue creative endeavors with passion and enthusiasm. Research suggests that environments that support autonomy, encourage experimentation, and provide opportunities for skill development foster intrinsic motivation and creativity.

Additionally, creativity is influenced by environmental factors such as organizational culture, social norms, and collaborative networks. Creativity thrives in environments that encourage risk-taking, tolerate failure, and value diverse perspectives and ideas. Organizational cultures that prioritize innovation, foster psychological safety, and provide resources for experimentation and learning cultivate a fertile ground for creativity and innovation to flourish.

Moreover, psychological research suggests that certain personality traits, such as openness to experience, curiosity, and persistence, are associated with higher levels of creativity. Openness to experience involves a willingness to explore new ideas, seek out new experiences, and challenge conventional wisdom, fostering a broad-minded and innovative approach to problem-solving. Curiosity drives individuals to ask questions, explore possibilities, and seek out novel solutions, fueling the creative process. Persistence involves the willingness to persevere in the face of setbacks, obstacles, or criticism, enabling individuals to overcome challenges and bring creative ideas to fruition.

In summary, creativity and innovation are multifaceted processes influenced by cognitive, emotional, and environmental factors. By understanding the psychological perspectives on creativity, individuals and organizations can cultivate environments and mindsets that support creative thinking and innovative problem-solving. By fostering a culture of curiosity, experimentation, and collaboration, we can harness the power of creativity to drive positive change and inspire innovation in all aspects of life.

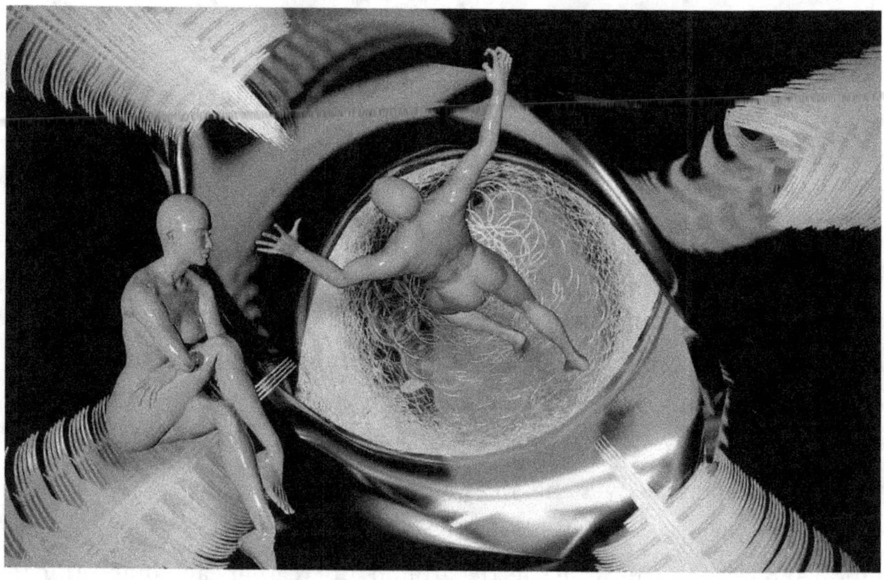

29

29

Spirituality and Psychological Growth

Spirituality is a deeply personal and multifaceted aspect of human experience that encompasses beliefs, values, practices, and experiences related to the search for meaning, purpose, and connection to something greater than oneself. While spirituality is often associated with religious traditions, it can also be expressed in secular forms and may involve exploring existential questions, cultivating inner peace, or seeking transcendence beyond the material world. Psychological research suggests that spirituality plays a significant role in promoting psychological growth, resilience, and well-being across the lifespan.

One way spirituality contributes to psychological growth is by providing individuals with a sense of meaning and purpose in life. Spiritually-oriented beliefs and practices help individuals make sense of their experiences, cope with adversity, and navigate existential questions such as the nature of existence, suffering, and death. By finding meaning in life's challenges and setbacks, individuals can experience a greater sense of coherence, resilience, and psychological well-being.

Moreover, spirituality fosters a sense of connection and belongingness, both to oneself, others, and the world at large. Spiritual practices such as meditation, prayer, and mindfulness cultivate awareness, compassion, and empathy, fostering deeper connections with oneself and others. Research suggests that individuals who report higher levels of spiritual well-being tend to have greater social support, healthier relationships, and a stronger sense of community, all of which contribute to psychological growth and well-being.

Furthermore, spirituality promotes inner peace, emotional regulation, and resilience in the face of stress, trauma, and adversity. Spiritual practices such as meditation, mindfulness, and prayer have been shown to reduce stress, anxiety, and depressive symptoms, promoting emotional well-being and psychological resilience. By cultivating a sense of inner peace and acceptance, individuals can navigate life's challenges with greater equanimity and grace, fostering psychological growth and well-being.

Additionally, spirituality fosters personal growth and self-transcendence by encouraging individuals to transcend egoic concerns and cultivate qualities such as compassion, forgiveness, and gratitude. Spiritual practices such as acts of kindness, service to others, and self-reflection promote personal growth and self-awareness, leading to greater empathy, wisdom, and humility. By transcending self-centered concerns and cultivating a sense of interconnectedness with all beings, individuals can experience a profound sense of spiritual fulfillment and psychological growth.

Moreover, spirituality can provide a sense of hope, resilience, and optimism in the face of suffering, loss, and uncertainty. Beliefs in a higher power, divine providence, or cosmic order can offer solace, comfort, and reassurance during difficult times, fostering resilience and hope in the midst of adversity. By drawing upon spiritual resources such as faith, prayer, and community support, individuals can find strength and meaning in the midst of life's challenges, promoting psychological growth and well-being.

In summary, spirituality plays a significant role in promoting psychological growth, resilience, and well-being by providing individuals with a sense of meaning, connection, inner peace, and transcendence. By cultivating spiritual practices and beliefs that resonate with their values and aspirations, individuals can enhance their psychological well-being, deepen their sense of purpose, and experience greater fulfillment and flourishing in life. Spirituality offers a pathway to psychological growth and transformation, enabling individuals to cultivate resilience, wisdom, and compassion in the journey toward self-discovery and self-actualization.

Spirituality encompasses a deeply personal and often transcendent connection to something greater than oneself, whether it be a higher power, the universe, nature, or the interconnectedness of all beings. While spirituality is often associated with religious beliefs and practices, it can also exist independently as a source of meaning, purpose, and inner fulfillment. Psychological research suggests that spirituality can play a significant role in promoting psychological growth, resilience, and well-being across the lifespan.

One way spirituality fosters psychological growth is by providing individuals with a sense of meaning and purpose in life. Spiritual beliefs and values help individuals make sense of their experiences, find direction and guidance in times of uncertainty, and navigate life's challenges with greater resilience and equanimity. Research has shown that individuals who report a strong sense of spiritual meaning and purpose tend to experience greater life satisfaction, happiness, and overall well-being.

Moreover, spirituality is often associated with practices such as meditation, prayer, mindfulness, and contemplation, which have been shown to promote psychological growth and well-being. These practices cultivate qualities such as self-awareness, emotional regulation, and compassion, leading to greater inner peace, clarity, and contentment. Mindfulness-based interventions, for example, have been found to reduce stress, anxiety, and depression while enhancing overall psychological well-being.

Furthermore, spirituality fosters a sense of interconnectedness and compassion toward others, promoting prosocial behavior, empathy, and altruism. Spiritual values such as love, kindness, forgiveness, and gratitude inspire individuals to extend care and support to others, fostering deeper connections and relationships. Research has shown that individuals who report higher levels of spiritual well-being tend to exhibit greater empathy, compassion, and social connectedness, contributing to their overall psychological growth and well-being.

Additionally, spirituality can serve as a source of resilience and coping in the face of adversity and trauma. Spiritual beliefs and practices provide individuals with a sense of hope, comfort, and inner strength during times of crisis or loss. Faith in a higher power or belief in the inherent goodness of humanity can offer solace and perspective, enabling individuals to find meaning and purpose in their suffering and to transcend their pain through acts of forgiveness, acceptance, and healing.

Moreover, spirituality encourages individuals to cultivate virtues such as humility, gratitude, and acceptance, which are associated with greater psychological well-being and resilience. Humility involves recognizing one's limitations, imperfections, and interconnectedness with others, fostering a sense of humility and openness to learning and growth. Gratitude involves appreciating the blessings and opportunities in one's life, leading to greater feelings of contentment, joy, and satisfaction. Acceptance involves embracing life's imperfections, uncertainties, and paradoxes with equanimity and grace, leading to greater inner peace and resilience in the face of life's challenges.

In summary, spirituality plays a multifaceted role in promoting psychological growth, resilience, and well-being. By providing individuals with a sense of meaning, purpose, and connection to something greater than oneself, spirituality fosters inner peace, compassion, and resilience in the face of adversity. By cultivating spiritual practices and values such as mindfulness, compassion, and gratitude, individuals can deepen their sense of spiritual well-being and enhance their overall psychological growth and flourishing.

30

30

Mental Health and Psychological Growth

Mental health and psychological growth are closely intertwined, with psychological growth often serving as a pathway to improved mental health and well-being. Psychological growth encompasses the process of self-discovery, personal development, and resilience-building that occurs in response to life's challenges and experiences. By nurturing psychological growth, individuals can cultivate the skills, strengths, and resources needed to navigate adversity, promote mental health, and foster overall well-being.

One aspect of psychological growth involves developing self-awareness and insight into one's thoughts, feelings, and behaviors. Through self-reflection, therapy, or mindfulness practices, individuals can gain a deeper understanding of their emotional triggers, cognitive patterns, and underlying beliefs, empowering them to make positive changes and overcome obstacles to mental health.

Moreover, psychological growth involves cultivating adaptive coping strategies and resilience-building skills to cope with stress, adversity, and life transitions. Resilience—the ability to bounce back from setbacks, adapt to change, and thrive in the face of adversity—is a key factor in promoting mental health and well-being. By fostering resilience through practices such as cognitive reframing, problem-solving, and social support, individuals can develop the capacity to navigate life's challenges with greater ease and effectiveness.

Furthermore, psychological growth encompasses the development of positive relationships and social connections that contribute to mental health and well-being. Strong social support networks, nurturing relationships, and a sense of belonging promote emotional resilience, reduce feelings of loneliness and isolation, and provide a source of comfort and validation during difficult times. By cultivating healthy relationships and seeking support from others, individuals can enhance their mental health and overall quality of life.

Additionally, psychological growth involves fostering a sense of purpose, meaning, and fulfillment in life—a key component of mental health and well-being. Engaging in activities that align with one's values, interests, and aspirations promotes a sense of purpose and satisfaction, contributing to overall life satisfaction and psychological well-being. By pursuing meaningful goals, engaging in creative pursuits, or giving back to others through acts of kindness or service, individuals can enhance their sense of purpose and fulfillment in life.

Furthermore, psychological growth is facilitated by practices that promote self-care, stress management, and holistic well-being. Activities such as exercise, nutrition, sleep hygiene, and relaxation techniques support mental health by reducing stress, improving mood, and enhancing overall well-being. By prioritizing self-care and adopting healthy lifestyle habits, individuals can support their psychological growth and resilience, leading to improved mental health and quality of life.

In summary, mental health and psychological growth are interconnected processes that support and reinforce each other. By fostering self-awareness, resilience, positive relationships, meaning, and self-care practices, individuals can cultivate psychological growth and promote mental health and well-being. Embracing psychological growth as a pathway to mental health empowers individuals to thrive, flourish, and lead fulfilling lives despite life's challenges and adversities.

Mental health is not merely the absence of mental illness but encompasses a state of well-being in which individuals can realize their own potential, cope with life's stressors, work productively, and contribute to their communities. Psychological growth is an integral aspect of mental health, involving continuous development, adaptation, and resilience in the face of challenges and life transitions. By fostering psychological growth, individuals can enhance their mental health and overall well-being.

One way mental health promotes psychological growth is by providing a foundation for resilience and coping in the face of adversity. Individuals with good mental health are better equipped to navigate life's challenges, setbacks, and stressors, drawing upon internal and external resources to cope effectively and bounce back from setbacks. Resilience—the ability to adapt and thrive in the face of adversity—is a key component of psychological growth, enabling individuals to learn from setbacks, develop new skills, and find meaning and purpose in difficult experiences.

Moreover, mental health promotes psychological growth by fostering self-awareness, self-acceptance, and personal development. Individuals with good mental health are more likely to have a positive self-image, realistic self-esteem, and a sense of self-efficacy—the belief in one's ability to overcome challenges and achieve goals. By cultivating self-awareness and self-acceptance, individuals can identify their strengths, values, and goals, leading to greater authenticity, fulfillment, and psychological growth.

Furthermore, mental health supports psychological growth by fostering healthy relationships and social connections. Positive social support networks provide individuals with emotional validation, encouragement, and practical assistance during times of need, buffering against the effects of stress and adversity. Healthy relationships promote empathy, compassion, and mutual growth, enabling individuals to learn from others, develop interpersonal skills, and cultivate a sense of belonging and connection.

Additionally, mental health facilitates psychological growth by fostering a sense of purpose, meaning, and fulfillment in life. Individuals with good mental health are more likely to have clear goals, values, and priorities that provide direction and motivation in life. By pursuing meaningful activities, engaging in personal growth endeavors, and contributing to others, individuals can cultivate a sense of purpose and fulfillment that promotes psychological growth and well-being.

Moreover, mental health enables individuals to engage in practices that promote psychological growth, such as mindfulness, self-care, and lifelong learning. Mindfulness practices cultivate present-moment awareness, acceptance, and compassion, fostering resilience and emotional well-being. Self-care practices such as exercise, adequate sleep, and stress management promote physical and mental health, enabling individuals to thrive and grow. Lifelong learning fosters curiosity, creativity, and intellectual growth, enriching individuals' lives and expanding their horizons.

In summary, mental health is closely intertwined with psychological growth, fostering resilience, self-awareness, social connections, and a sense of purpose and fulfillment. By promoting mental health through proactive self-care, positive relationships, and engagement in meaningful activities, individuals can enhance their psychological growth and overall well-being. Embracing mental health as a foundation for growth and flourishing enables individuals to realize their full potential and lead fulfilling, meaningful lives.

31

31

Conclusion: Reflections on Lifelong Growth and Development

The journey of life is a continuous process of growth, development, and transformation. From infancy to old age, individuals navigate a myriad of experiences, challenges, and opportunities that shape their personalities, perspectives, and paths in life. Reflecting on the theme of lifelong growth and development, it becomes evident that every stage of life offers unique possibilities for learning, adaptation, and personal evolution.

Throughout the lifespan, individuals encounter various milestones, transitions, and turning points that catalyze growth and transformation. Childhood is a time of exploration, discovery, and identity formation, as individuals develop foundational skills, values, and relationships that shape their future trajectories. Adolescence brings a period of self-discovery, identity exploration, and autonomy-seeking, as individuals navigate the complexities of adolescence and begin to envision their roles and aspirations in adulthood.

Adulthood is characterized by a multitude of roles, responsibilities, and life transitions, as individuals pursue education, careers, relationships, and personal goals. It is a time of consolidation, achievement, and self-actualization, as individuals strive to realize their full potential and make meaningful contributions to society. Moreover, adulthood offers opportunities for personal growth, self-discovery, and reinvention, as individuals adapt to changing circumstances, pursue new interests, and explore new avenues for fulfillment and satisfaction.

In later adulthood, individuals confront the realities of aging, retirement, and reflection on life's accomplishments and regrets. It is a time of wisdom, reflection, and legacy-building, as individuals draw upon their life experiences, relationships, and values to find meaning, purpose, and fulfillment in later life. Despite the challenges of aging, older adults often demonstrate remarkable resilience, adaptability, and growth, as they embrace new roles, pursue lifelong learning, and continue to contribute to their communities and the world around them.

Reflecting on the theme of lifelong growth and development, it is clear that growth is not confined to any specific stage of life but is an ongoing and dynamic process that unfolds across the lifespan. It is a journey of self-discovery, learning, and adaptation, as individuals navigate the highs and lows of life with courage, resilience, and optimism. Lifelong growth and development are not only about achieving external milestones or accomplishments but also about cultivating inner wisdom, resilience, and compassion that enrich our lives and the lives of others.

As we journey through life, may we embrace the opportunities for growth and development that each stage brings, recognizing that every experience, challenge, and relationship has the potential to teach us valuable lessons and deepen our understanding of ourselves and the world around us. May we approach life with curiosity, openness, and a willingness to learn, knowing that the journey of growth and development is not a destination but a lifelong adventure filled with possibilities, discoveries, and opportunities for personal and collective evolution.

Lifelong growth and development are fundamental aspects of the human experience, characterized by continuous learning, adaptation, and transformation across the lifespan. As we journey through life, we encounter a myriad of experiences, challenges, and opportunities that shape who we are and who we become. From infancy to old age, each stage of life offers unique opportunities for growth, self-discovery, and personal fulfillment.

Throughout our lives, we undergo physical, cognitive, emotional, and social changes that challenge us to adapt and evolve. From the formative years of childhood and adolescence to the complexities of adulthood and the wisdom of old age, each stage presents its own set of joys, struggles, and milestones. By embracing the inevitability of change and uncertainty, we open ourselves up to the possibility of growth, resilience, and self-transformation.

One of the key themes that emerge from reflections on lifelong growth and development is the importance of resilience—the ability to bounce back from setbacks, overcome adversity, and thrive in the face of challenges. Resilience enables us to navigate life's ups and downs with courage, strength, and optimism, allowing us to learn from our experiences, build on our strengths, and persevere in the pursuit of our goals and aspirations.

Moreover, lifelong growth and development are fueled by curiosity, creativity, and a willingness to embrace new experiences and perspectives. By remaining open-minded, curious, and adaptable, we can continue to learn, grow, and evolve throughout our lives. Whether it's exploring new hobbies, learning new skills, or challenging ourselves to step outside our comfort zones, each new experience has the potential to enrich our lives and expand our horizons.

Furthermore, lifelong growth and development are nurtured by meaningful connections with others and a sense of belonging to something greater than ourselves. Human beings are inherently social creatures, and our relationships with family, friends, and communities play a crucial role in shaping who we are and who we become. By fostering empathy, compassion, and mutual support in our relationships, we create environments that promote growth, well-being, and collective flourishing.

As we reflect on the journey of lifelong growth and development, we are reminded of the inherent resilience, creativity, and potential that lies within each of us. Regardless of our age or circumstances, we have the power to cultivate resilience, pursue growth, and embrace the opportunities for learning and self-discovery that life presents. By embracing the journey of lifelong growth and development with courage, curiosity, and an open heart, we can live more fully, authentically, and meaningfully, enriching our lives and the lives of those around us.

As we reflect on the journey of lifelong growth and development, it becomes evident that the human experience is a dynamic and ever-evolving process. From infancy to old age, individuals are constantly growing, learning, and adapting to the challenges and opportunities that life presents. Throughout this journey, various factors—biological, psychological, social, and environmental—shape our development and contribute to who we become.

One of the key themes that emerges from this exploration is the importance of resilience in the face of adversity. Life is filled with ups and downs, successes and setbacks, yet it is our ability to bounce back from adversity, learn from our experiences, and grow stronger that ultimately defines our journey. Resilience enables us to navigate life's challenges with courage, grace, and optimism, allowing us to persevere in the face of obstacles and setbacks.

Another theme that emerges is the significance of relationships and social connections in fostering growth and well-being. From the earliest stages of life, our relationships with caregivers, peers, and communities shape our development and contribute to our sense of belonging and connection. Throughout life, positive relationships provide us with support, encouragement, and a sense of shared humanity that enriches our lives and promotes our growth and well-being.

Moreover, this exploration underscores the importance of self-awareness and self-acceptance in fostering personal growth and fulfillment. By cultivating a deep understanding of ourselves—our strengths, weaknesses, values, and aspirations—we can navigate life with authenticity, integrity, and purpose. Self-acceptance allows us to embrace our imperfections, celebrate our uniqueness, and find meaning and fulfillment in our journey of self-discovery.

Furthermore, the journey of lifelong growth and development is characterized by a continual process of learning, adaptation, and transformation. Life presents us with endless opportunities for growth—in our careers, relationships, personal pursuits, and spiritual journeys. By remaining open-minded, curious, and receptive to new experiences and perspectives, we can continue to evolve and expand our horizons throughout life.

In conclusion, the journey of lifelong growth and development is a remarkable and transformative odyssey filled with challenges, opportunities, and moments of profound insight and discovery. As we navigate this journey, may we embrace the principles of resilience, relationships, self-awareness, and lifelong learning to cultivate a life of meaning, purpose, and fulfillment. By embracing the journey of growth with courage, curiosity, and compassion, we can unlock our full potential and live lives of joy, authenticity, and fulfillment.

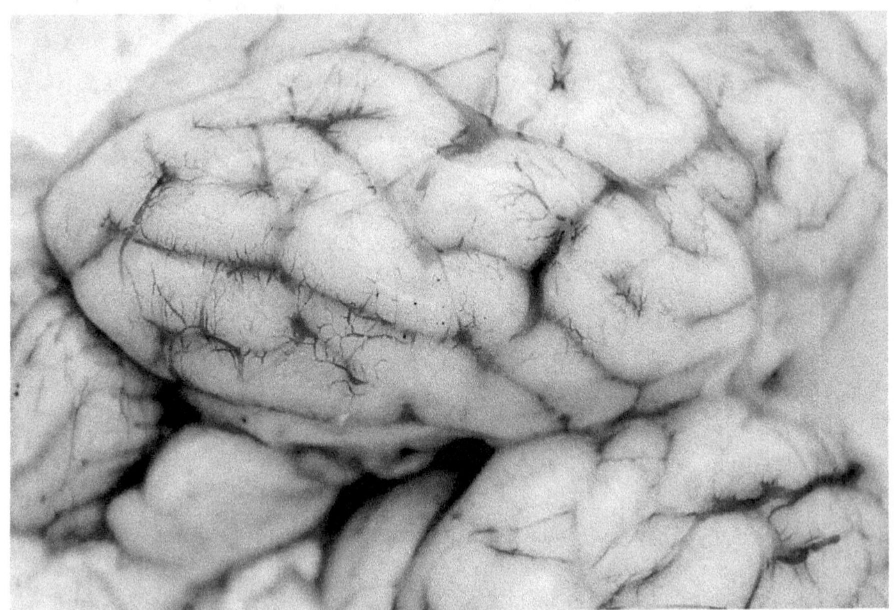

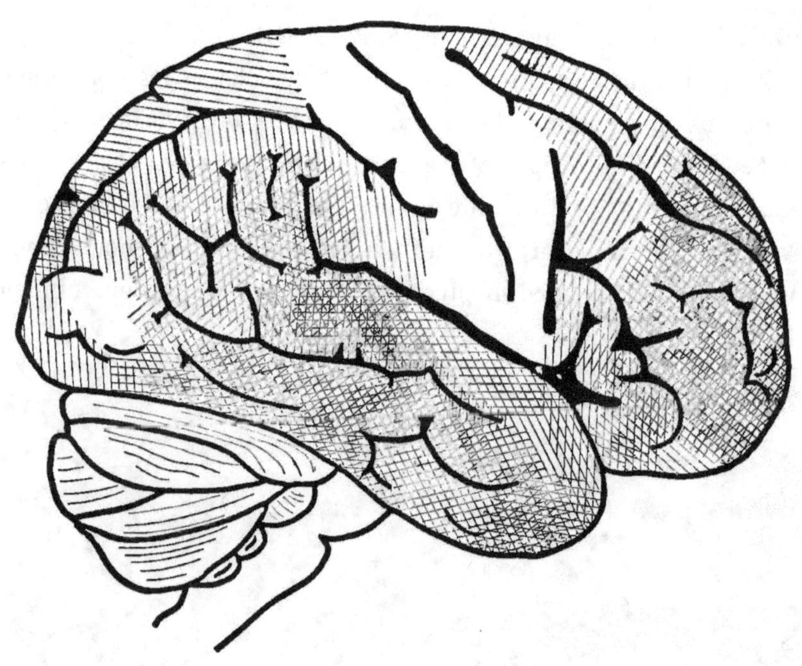

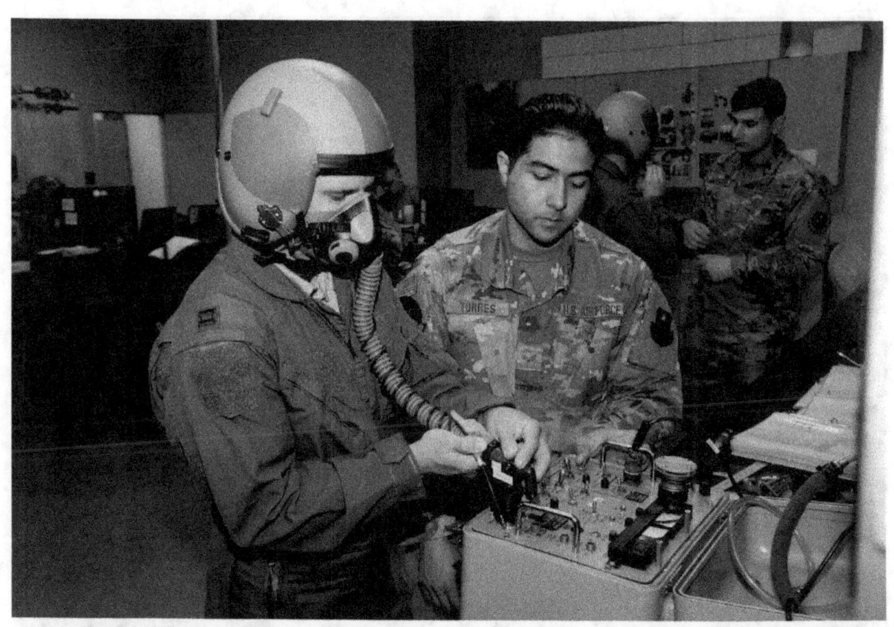

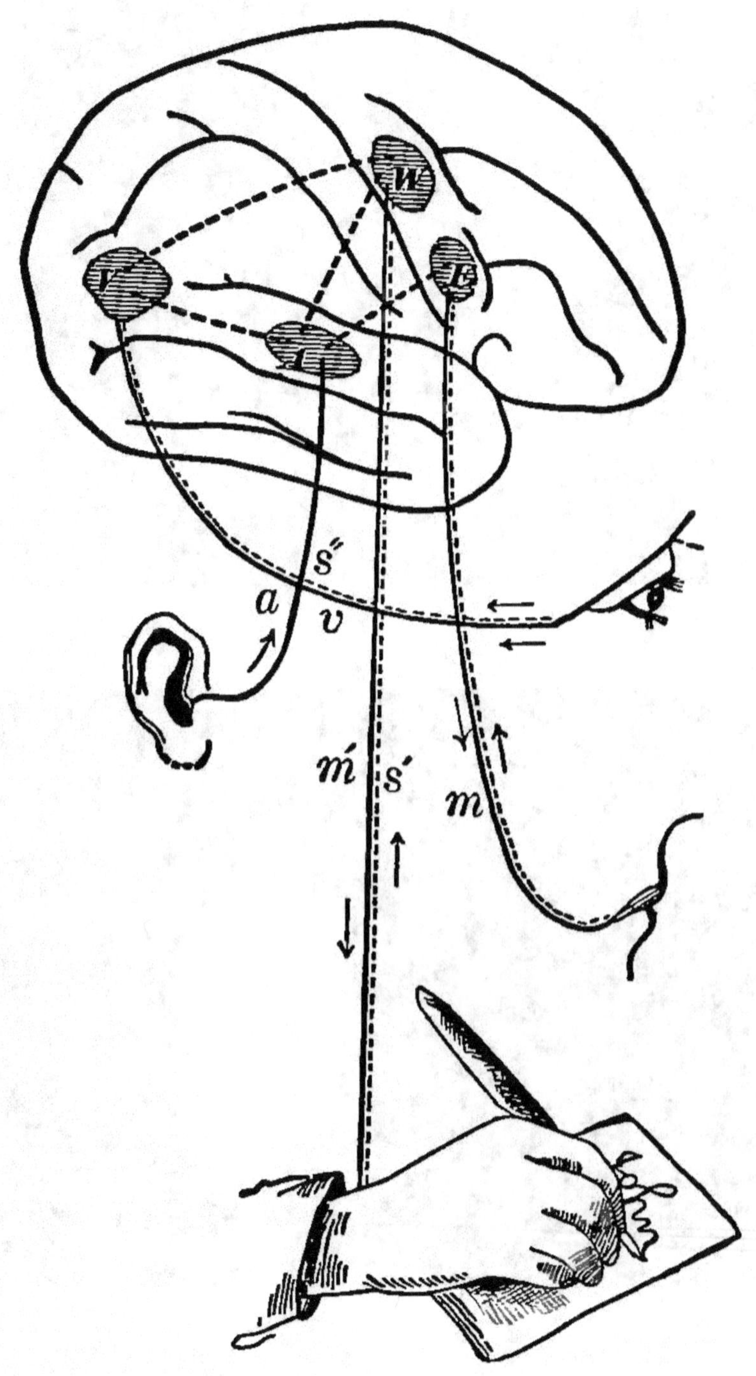

w
a
s̈
v
m̀
s̀
m

FAMILIE
FAMILIE

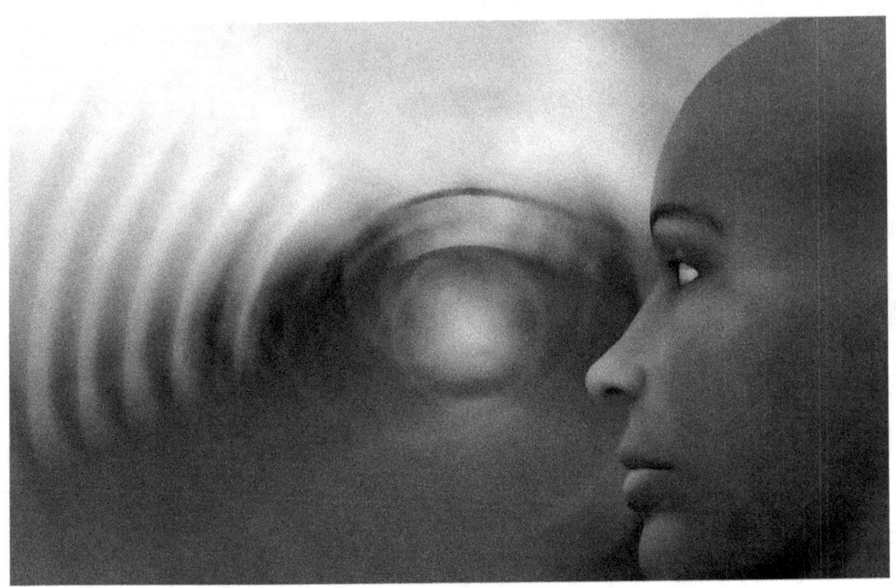

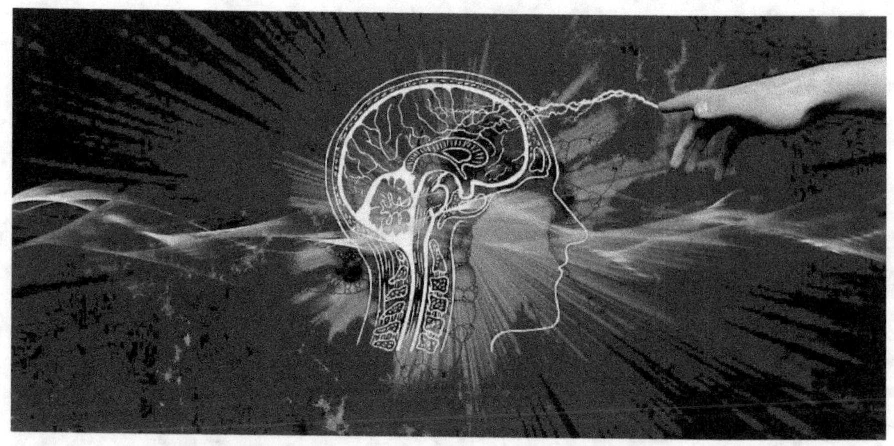